Reading FORWARD

ADVANCED 2

Reading FORWARD

ADVANCED 2

Series Editors Bin-na Yang, Dong-sook Kim

Project Editors Jung-ah Lee, Mina Song, Mi-youn Woo, Jee-young Song, Kyung-hee Kim, Na-hyun Ahn, Eun-kyung Kim

Contributing Writers Patrick Ferraro, Henry John Amen IV, John Boswell, Robert Vernon, Keeran Murphy, Peter Morton

Illustrators Seol-hee Kim, Hyun-il Bang, Hyun-jin Choi, Hyo-sil Lee

Design Hyun-jung Jang, Yeon-joo Kim

Editorial Designer In-sun Lee

Sales Ki-young Han, Kyung-koo Lee, In-gyu Park, Cheol-gyo Jeong, Nam-jun Kim, Nam-hyung Kim, Woo-hyun Lee

Marketers Hye-sun Park, Yu-jin Ko, Yeo-jin Kim

ISBN 979-11-253-0801-0 53740

INTRODUCTION

★
★
★

Reading Forward is a six-level series of three progressive steps: Basic, Intermediate, and Advanced. Based on the essential needs of young students, the series focuses on a specific goal: expanding vocabulary and knowledge. This goal guides all of the content and activities in the series. The first step of the series will enlarge vocabulary, and the later steps will increase knowledge. Thus, the series will eventually help students improve their reading comprehension.

Each book of Reading Forward is composed of 20 units. The number of words used in each reading passage is as follows.

Step 3
Reading Forward
Advanced
for Knowledge
1 : 240 – 260 words
2 : 260 – 280 words

Step 2
Reading Forward
Intermediate
for Vocabulary & Knowledge
1 : 200 – 220 words
2 : 220 – 240 words

Step 1
Reading Forward
Basic
for Vocabulary
1 : 150 – 170 words
2 : 170 – 190 words

Key Features of Reading Forward Series

– Current, high-interest topics are developed in an easy way so that students can understand them. These subjects can hold their attention and keep them motivated to read forward.

– Comprehension checkup questions presented in the series are based on standardized test questions. These can help students prepare for English tests at school, as well as official English language tests.

– Each unit is designed to expand knowledge by presenting a further reading passage related to the main topic. Students will build their background knowledge which helps improve their reading comprehension.

FORMAT

Before Reading
The question before each passage allows students to think about the topic by relating it to their lives. It also helps students become interested in the passage before reading it.

Reading
This part serves as the main passage of the unit, and it explains an intriguing and instructive topic in great depth. As students progress through the book, the content of these passages becomes more and more substantial.

Reading Comprehension
The reading is followed by different types of questions, which test understanding of the passage. The various types of questions focus on important reading skills, such as understanding the main idea and organization of the passage, identifying details, and drawing inferences.

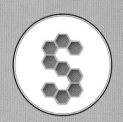

Strategic Summary / Organizer

Each unit includes a strategic summary or organizer of the main reading passage. It gives students a better understanding of the important points and organization of the passage. These exercises focus on further development of effective reading comprehension skills.

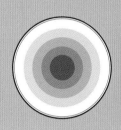

Knowledge Expanding

Each unit provides a shorter reading passage related to the topic of the main passage. It elaborates on the content of the main passage by providing additional information or examples, further explanation, or a different point of view on the subject.

Vocabulary Review

A review of the key vocabulary concludes each unit. Three types of exercises test understanding of new words: matching definitions, identifying synonyms and antonyms, and completing sentences with the correct words in context.

TABLE OF CONTENTS

★ ★ ★ ★ ★

Reading Forward

The U.S. Dollar Coin

If you have any coins or bills with you, take a close look at the front of one. Who appears there? Generally, the figures selected to appear on currency are considered

5 important by the people of a country, and often they were famous leaders, like Queen Elizabeth II in the U.K. or King Sejong in Korea. However, America has done something different with its $1 coin.

10 The Sacagawea dollar coin is worth $1, and it features an image of a 15-year-old Native American girl. It has been issued since 2000, along with special presidential coins. (①) But there is one more thing that makes it special. (②) In 2007, the Native American $1 Coin Act was passed to further honor Native American history. (③) Each

15 year during this period, the back of the coin will feature a different image, depicting themes related to various Native American tribes. (④)

But what makes Sacagawea so important to Americans? Though only a teenager, she knew several Indian languages and was familiar with many native tribes. For these reasons, she was hired by the historic Lewis and

20 Clark Expedition, which explored the Western U.S. from 1804 to 1806. Sacagawea successfully guided Lewis and Clark along their journey from the Northern Great Plains to the Pacific Ocean and back. Without her help, the explorers surely would have died.

Strangely, no one knows _____(A)_____.
She died at the age of 25, and no picture or description of her has ever been found. The image on the coin was based on a Native American model of roughly the same age and background. Although the image is not entirely accurate, it still represents a wonderful piece of American history!

1 What is the passage mainly about?

   a. The various designs of U.S. dollar coins

   b. The special dollar coin honoring Native Americans

   c. The historic expedition that appears on a U.S. dollar coin

   d. The high standard of choosing a model for the U.S. dollar coins

2 Where would the following sentence best fit?

The act called for special Sacagawea coins to be produced through the 2010s.

   a. ①   *b.* ②   *c.* ③   *d.* ④

3 What are the traits of the Sacagawea dollar coin? (Choose two.)

   a. The figure on the coin is an ordinary person.

   b. The image on the back changes regularly.

   c. It is the only dollar coin issued in the U.S.

   d. It was designed by a Native American girl.

4 Why did Lewis and Clark hire Sacagawea for their expedition?

   _____

5 What is the best choice for blank (A)?

   a. how Sacagawea died

   b. what Sacagawea really looked like

   c. why Sacagawea helped the expedition

   d. whether Sacagawea was paid for her work

6 What is NOT true according to the passage?

   a. The Sacagawea coin is still produced today.

   b. The Sacagawea coins were made to replace the presidential coins.

   c. Sacagawea acted as a guide for the Lewis and Clark Expedition.

   d. The face on the Sacagawea coin was modeled by another person.

Fill in the blanks with the correct words.

Countries often put images of their past _____ on their money. The U.S. dollar coin, on the other hand, features the image of a young Native American woman, Sacagawea. She _____ the Lewis and Clark Expedition from 1804 to 1806. The coin, which will be produced through the 2010s, will feature on its back a _____ image related to a Native American tribe each year. Interestingly, there is no _____ of what Sacagawea actually looked like. The image on the coin is based on a girl of approximately the same age and _____.

guided	record	bills	background	different	leaders

★ EXPANDING KNOWLEDGE ★

The most common form of U.S. currency is the dollar bill, which was first produced in 1862. The dollar bill is worth $1, and it has featured George Washington, the first president of the United States, since 1869. Prior to the release of the dollar bill, the dollar was a coin that originally appeared in 1794. Today, there are several different dollar coins in circulation. The oldest among them is the Susan B. Anthony coin. It has been around since 1979 and features the image of the famous female social activist for whom it is named. It is still available but no longer produced. People often confused the coin with the similar looking quarter, so the government therefore made all later dollar coins gold in color. These include the presidential dollar coins honoring former U.S. presidents and the Native American coin also known as the Sacagawea coin. These dollar coins are all currently used along with the dollar bill.

1 What is the passage mainly about?

   a. The types of U.S. dollars   *b.* The value of the U.S. dollar

   c. The history of the U.S. dollar bill   *d.* The U.S. dollar as international currency

2 What is NOT true according to the passage?

   a. The dollar bill is more widely used than dollar coins in the U.S.

   b. The dollar coin was released earlier than the dollar bill.

   c. The Susan B. Anthony coin is completely out of circulation now.

   d. The presidential dollar coins are gold in color.

VOCABULARY REVIEW

A Write the correct word next to its definition.

| description | currency | theme | figure | feature |

1 to include something as an important part: _____

2 the type of money used in a particular country: _____

3 someone who is important or well known in some way: _____

4 a piece of writing or speech about what someone or something is like: _____

B Complete each sentence with a word in the box. (Change the form if needed.)

| honor | historic | prior to | presidential | accurate | issue | expedition |

1 The _____ event was broadcast live all over the world.

2 I broke up with my boyfriend three days _____ my birthday.

3 Barack Obama won the U.S. _____ election in November 2008.

4 Last summer, I was given the chance to go on a(n) _____ in Africa.

5 We are here to _____ all the people who fought for women's rights.

6 The magazine is _____ once a month and can also be purchased online.

C Find the word that has a similar meaning to the underlined word.

1 In some stories, she is depicted as a beautiful woman with brown hair.

a. described   b. known   c. recommended   d. remembered

2 I've told you roughly how much it will cost.

a. lately   b. confidently   c. approximately   d. exactly

ENTERTAINMENT

Movie Posters

The use of posters to promote movies is an old tradition, but in the 21st century, posters really have to stand out to make an impact. Otherwise, they'll be overlooked as just another part of

5 the commercial background of our lives. When designing a poster, designers try to create an image that both intrigues viewers and gives them some facts about the movie.

Movie posters usually belong to one of

10 three styles. The first is the *teaser poster. Teasers don't offer much information; instead, they feature an interesting scene or tag line from the film that makes us want to learn more. Another common style is the character poster, which focuses on an image of the film's main character.

15 The poster for the movie *300* demonstrates this style. It shows the main character dressed for battle and yelling at his enemies. Finally, there are artistic posters. These are more abstract and attempt to illustrate the theme or feeling of the movie through an artistic image.

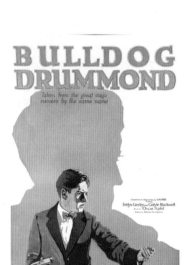

Regardless of a poster's type, it usually gives us clues to the movie's _____(A)_____. For instance, the poster for a superhero film looks very different from one for a romantic comedy. If you see a poster with a dark, lonesome house on a spooky hill at night, and its text is written in a wavy, ghostly style, you know it's advertising a horror movie.

It's clear that <u>movie posters are more than just promotions</u>. Their main goal is to capture our attention and encourage us to see the film. But they also need to provide hints about the film's content without giving away its secrets. That's hard to do with a single image!

*teaser: an ad that makes people interested by not giving much information

1 What is the passage mainly about?

    a. Current movie poster trends

    b. The history of movie posters

    c. The genres and roles of movie posters

    d. The qualifications of a good film poster

2 What do designers try to do when they design a movie poster?

3 What is NOT true about movie posters?

    a. Most movie posters come in one of three types.

    b. A teaser poster excites viewers' curiosity about a movie.

    c. A character poster features an impressive image of an actor.

    d. An artistic poster shows the most beautiful scene in the movie.

4 What is the best choice for blank (A)?

    a. title   *b.* director

    c. genre   *d.* purpose

5 What does the underlined part mean?

    a. Movie posters should satisfy artistic requirements.

    b. The success of a movie depends on its promotional poster.

    c. Movie posters should contain information about filmmaking.

    d. The subject matter of a movie can be guessed from the posters.

6 Write T if the statement is true or F if it's false.

    1) Posters have been used to advertise movies for a long time.

    2) The text style of a poster sometimes gives a hint about its film's genre.

Fill in the blanks with the correct words.

Movie Posters

Types	• Teaser posters: focus on a scene or tag line from the movie that will _____ viewers
	• Character posters: feature a main character from the movie
	• Artistic posters: show the theme or feeling of a movie in a(n) _____ manner
	→ Regardless of its type, each poster indicates the movie's _____.
Roles	• Catch people's _____ so they will want to see the movie
	• _____ about the film without giving anything away

> hint   interest   genre   superhero   abstract   attention

★ EXPANDING KNOWLEDGE ★

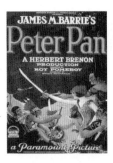

In the early days of film, movie posters were seen as nothing more than advertising material. A limited number were produced for each film, and the production studio would require that the theater return the posters after the film's run had ended.

After World War II, though, serious film fans began showing great interest in collecting the posters from their favorite movies. Recognizing their potential value, some theater owners started ignoring studios' return policies, saving a small number of vintage posters from the landfill. Subsequently, the classic "one sheet" poster was transformed into the most renowned film souvenir a collector could possess. Since the 1980s, such collections have gained international prestige, with the most expensive collections worth millions of dollars.

1 What is the passage mainly about?

   a. Political uses for movie posters
   b. The movie advertising business
   c. The history of collecting movie posters
   d. Evaluating the value of vintage posters

2 What is NOT true about movie posters before World War II?

   a. Advertising a film was the only purpose for producing them.
   b. Just a small number were made for each film.
   c. They were returned to the distributor after showing the film.
   d. Some rare movie posters drew the attention of movie fans.

VOCABULARY REVIEW

A Write the correct word next to its definition.

souvenir	intrigue	potential	overlook	prestige

1 to fail to notice or consider something: _____

2 to make someone very interested in something: _____

3 having the possibility to exist or develop in the future: _____

4 something that reminds someone of a special event or place: _____

B Complete each sentence with a word in the box. (Change the form if needed.)

illustrate	worth	regardless of	promote	yell at	transform	abstract

1 At night, this café is _____ into a restaurant.

2 The paintings represent _____ ideas, such as truth and justice.

3 This is a club that anyone can join _____ age, race, or gender.

4 The band decided to go on a concert tour to _____ its album.

5 I stood up, turned around, and _____ them to stop kicking my chair.

6 The book contains three short stories to _____ three basic facts of life.

C Find the word that has a similar meaning to the underlined word.

1 The island is <u>renowned</u> for its fantastic beaches.

　　a. crowded　　　　*b.* unknown　　　　*c.* good　　　　*d.* famous

2 The police found an important <u>clue</u> to this case.

　　a. secret　　　　*b.* hint　　　　*c.* rule　　　　*d.* figure

Before Reading

Have you ever had the feeling of being watched by a portrait on the wall?

Eyes in Paintings

You are in the Louvre Museum in Paris to see the famous painting by Leonardo da Vinci called the *Mona Lisa*. As you view the woman in the painting,
5 you walk from side to side to see the details. But suddenly, you notice something rather scary. Wherever you move, the *Mona Lisa*'s eyes follow you! Has the painting come to life?

10 Of course, the *Mona Lisa* is not alive, but she was carefully painted to appear real. Da Vinci used a trick called perspective to do this. By painting certain parts of the image larger than
15 others, he made those sections appear "closer." The use of light and shadow has a similar effect, with lit areas seeming closer and those in shadow feeling farther away. These tools allow painters to create a sense of depth.

Yet, this depth is a sort of _____(A)_____. A canvas only
20 has two dimensions, compared to the three we see in the world around us. But when you look at your friend's face and move from side to side, do his or her eyes follow you? Of course they do not. (①) This is because your perspective is changing. (②) When you move around, you see your friend's eyes from different distances, and
25 the light and shadow on his or her face changes. (③) They are permanent and flat. (④) Because of this, if the painted face is looking at you from one angle, its eyes will gaze at you from every other angle.

So there is nothing scary or magical about a portrait's eyes. But paintings in haunted mansions are different. If you see their eyes following
30 you, you'd better run!

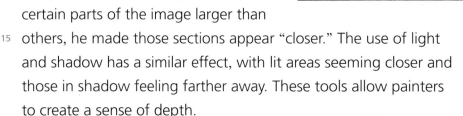

1 What is the passage mainly about?

   a. How to express distance in paintings

   b. How to draw a portrait that looks alive

   c. Why eyes in portraits seem to follow you

   d. Why the *Mona Lisa* is a great work of art

2 How does the writer introduce the topic?

   a. By defining a new concept in art

   b. By describing one of da Vinci's masterpieces

   c. By giving an example of the eyes in a portrait

   d. By suggesting a way of appreciating the artwork

3 How does the use of the techniques of perspective, light, and shadow affect paintings?

_____

4 What is the best choice for blank (A)?

   a. reality   *b.* illusion

   c. theory   *d.* symbol

5 Where would the following sentence best fit?

> However, in a painting, the qualities of perspective, light, and shadow are the same from every angle.

   a. ①   *b.* ②   *c.* ③   *d.* ④

6 Write T if the statement is true or F if it's false.

   1) Relative size can be used to make a painting look real.

   2) People tend to perceive dark colors as being close.

Fill in the blanks with the correct words.

STRATEGIC SUMMARY

You're looking at the *Mona Lisa* when you notice that her eyes keep following you. But they aren't really following you. They only seem to be. That's because da Vinci used a trick called _____. He painted some parts of the painting larger to make them look _____. However, since a painting is only two dimensional, this _____ is simply an illusion. The _____, unchanging images of a painting look the same from every perspective, making the eyes in a portrait appear to _____ you.

| follow | flat | depth | perspective | closer | gaze |

★ EXPANDING KNOWLEDGE ★

A large part of our understanding of the world is based on what we see. However, sometimes what we see is not what really exists. This incorrect perception of the world is called a visual illusion.

_____(A)_____ you may not realize it, you experience visual illusions almost every day. For instance, the millions of colors created by your television are the result of just three colors: red, green, and blue. If you look closely at the screen, you can see tiny dots containing these three colors. Because the colors are so close together, your brain combines them to produce countless other colors. Another common visual illusion is how patterns on clothes make a person look different. For example, clothes with vertical or horizontal stripes make a person look slimmer and taller.

So while we may believe that our eyes allow us to see reality, what we see is often different from the truth.

1 What is the best choice for blank (A)?

a. If   b. Because   c. Whenever   d. Although

2 What is NOT true according to the passage?

a. Our eyes provide an objective view of reality.
b. The colors on a TV screen are combinations of three colors.
c. The information gathered by the eye is processed in the brain.
d. Patterns can cause misrepresentations of size and length.

VOCABULARY REVIEW

A Write the correct word next to its definition.

portrait	perception	horizontal	visual	dimension

1 related to seeing: _____

2 straight and parallel to the ground: _____

3 a drawing, painting, or photograph of a person: _____

4 the ability to notice something by seeing, hearing, etc.: _____

B Complete each sentence with a word in the box. (Change the form if needed.)

flat	come to life	illusion	depth	angle	vertical	combine

1 Spring is the season when all living things _____.

2 Three cameras captured the scene from different _____.

3 The mirror in the room creates the _____ of greater space.

4 People who _____ diet with exercise will lose weight faster than others.

5 The painter drew a(n) _____ line from the top of the wall to the bottom.

6 An ice rink for a speed skating competition should be completely _____.

C Find the word that has a similar meaning to the underlined word.

1 The last part of the movie was quite scary.

    a. sad   *b.* beautiful   *c.* impressive   *d.* frightening

2 Your opinion is based on incorrect information.

    a. false   *b.* useful   *c.* reliable   *d.* complete

Stress

5

10

How do you feel during a difficult situation? Most likely, your heartbeat speeds up, your face gets warm, and you experience anxiety. This is a natural reaction. Your body is responding to the situation in a way to help you overcome it. But sometimes, the situation feels overwhelming, and that is when stress occurs.

Many things in our lives, from homework assignments to car accidents, can cause stress. _____(A)_____ we don't enjoy the

15 feeling, stress is not always negative. For example, if you're worried about finishing your homework, and stress makes you work faster and complete it on time, there is no problem. However, stress becomes negative rather than positive when you experience it continually for long periods. Such chronic stress is a serious health issue, and it must be dealt with.

20 One strategy for lowering stress is to simplify your daily to-do list. Figure out which tasks are urgent and which ones can wait. This will reduce your stress over non-essential activities. Another idea is to keep a journal. Write about situations that cause you stress, and then imagine all the possible outcomes of those situations. When you feel more prepared to face

25 them, you will be less stressed. Also, don't underestimate the importance of crying to release stress or adjusting your schedule to get more sleep. These physical strategies aid your body in handling a buildup of stress.

Test each of these stress-relieving methods to find the best one for you, or try creating your own! Once you discover what works, write it on a piece

30 of paper and put it on your desk or next to your bed. Whenever you feel stressed, look at your note and you will have the solution!

1 What is the passage mainly about?

    a. The effects of chronic stress

    b. Helpful ways to handle stress

    c. Many different types of stress

    d. The causes of stress in daily life

2 What is the best choice for blank (A)?

    a. Unless   *b.* Because

    c. Even though   *d.* As long as

3 Why does the writer mention homework?

    a. To suggest a way to get over stress

    b. To explain the positive effects of stress

    c. To show a common example of chronic stress

    d. To recommend a method of working efficiently

4 Writing about stressful situations and possible outcomes is helpful because

_____ .

5 What is NOT mentioned as a way to lower stress?

    a. Decide what to do first.

    b. Don't restrain yourself from crying.

    c. Make more time to sleep.

    d. Do some regular exercise.

6 Write T if the statement is true or F if it's false.

    1) When we are under stress, our body's reaction makes the situation worse.

    2) It is recommended that people try various methods for reducing stress.

STRATEGIC ORGANIZER

Fill in the blanks with the correct words.

Stress

Effects
- Positive: It helps increase your _____ to get things done.
- Negative: Chronic stress can be bad for your _____.

How to lower stress
- Make a list of daily activities and arrange it in order of _____.
- Keep a(n) _____ outlining your stressful situations and all their possible outcomes.
- Cry to release stress and get more _____.

importance   health   journal   sleep   ability   overcome

★ EXPANDING KNOWLEDGE ★

There are times in our lives when we face extremely stressful situations. These situations can have long-term effects on how our bodies and minds deal with stress and can lead to serious mental disorders, such as depression.

If your stress is too much for you to handle alone, you should definitely seek help. Talk to adults you can trust, such as your parents or a teacher. Be honest about the stress you are facing and how it is affecting you. This can make you feel less alone and allow you to find solutions to your problems. You may also want to receive counseling from a professional therapist, doctor, or religious leader. This can help you minimize the cause of your stress.

Understanding what your body tells you is an important part of growing up. Whenever you feel stressed out, remember that help is always available.

1 What is the writer's suggestion for addressing extreme stress?

a. Get plenty of rest.   b. Find a person to consult.
c. Try to understand yourself.   d. Find solutions on your own.

2 Write T if the statement is true or F if it's false.

1) Too much stress can cause mental illness.
2) When you deal with stress, you should be open about it.

VOCABULARY REVIEW

A Write the correct word next to its definition.

chronic	overwhelming	mental	underestimate	anxiety

1 so strong that it cannot be fought: _____

2 a worried feeling that something bad might happen: _____

3 lasting for a long time or happening again and again: _____

4 to think that something is less important than it really is: _____

B Complete each sentence with a word in the box. (Change the form if needed.)

release	respond	figure out	urgent	simplify	continually	reaction

1 Humor allows people to _____ stress.

2 He tried to _____ the story for the young audience.

3 Life is _____ changing. Nothing ever stays the same.

4 When I told him what happened, his initial _____ was to laugh.

5 In the past, people used telegrams to convey a(n) _____ message.

6 I think if we work together, we can _____ the answer to this question.

C Find the word that has a similar meaning to the underlined word.

1 He suffered from a rare underline{disorder} of the heart.

    a. illness   *b.* shape   *c.* movement   *d.* medicine

2 He tried to underline{minimize} the impact of his mistake.

    a. find   *b.* confess   *c.* face   *d.* reduce

Before Reading
Have you ever seen what soccer players do after a match?

Soccer Jersey Swap

Someone watching soccer for the first time might be surprised by what happens when the final whistle blows. After an intense contest, the players take off their jerseys and swap them with members of the opposing team. It may seem strange, but this has been a soccer tradition since 1931, when
5 players from France and England swapped shirts at the end of a match.

Why do players swap shirts with their opponents? (①) It is to show that, even though games are getting more intense these days, the spirit of fair play is still important. (②) For example, players from opposing teams help each other up after a foul. (③) Also, if an opponent gets
10 injured, the ball is kicked out of play so that he or she can receive medical treatment. (④) Likewise, swapping jerseys shows that the game is being played in a friendly and fair spirit.

The most famous jersey swap happened at the 1970 World Cup after Brazil's quarter-final victory over England. Brazil's greatest player ever, Pele, exchanged jerseys with England's greatest player ever, Bobby Moore. The sight of these two great champions trading shirts is perhaps the most famous image in soccer history. From that moment on, famous soccer stars like Pele needed more jerseys than other players since opposing players all wanted to swap jerseys with them.

Nowadays, jersey swapping happens at the end of every important match as an essential part of showing opponents friendship and respect. In fact, because of this, players are being supplied with extra jerseys!

1 What is the passage mainly about?

    a. The meaning of sportsmanship

    b. The background of a soccer tradition

    c. The history of change in uniform designs

    d. The popularity of soccer around the world

2 Where would the following sentence best fit?

> There are other similar traditions in soccer that you may have seen.

    a. ①   *b.* ②   *c.* ③   *d.* ④

3 What is NOT an action based on the spirit of fair play in soccer?

    a. Switching players during the game

    b. Exchanging jerseys with opposing players

    c. Helping an opposing player up after a hard tackle

    d. Kicking the ball out of play when an opponent gets hurt

4 Why did famous players like Pele need more jerseys than others?

_____

5 What is NOT mentioned about jersey swapping?

    a. When it began

    b. What it means

    c. What the most famous example of it is

    d. How significant it is for soccer fans

6 Write T if the statement is true or F if it's false.

    1) We can see jersey swapping when a soccer match is over.

    2) Pele and Bobby Moore were the first players to exchange jerseys.

Fill in the blanks with the correct words.

The tradition of swapping jerseys shows that the spirit of fair play remains _____ in soccer. The game has many examples of this, such as _____ an opponent up after a hard tackle. Similarly, swapping jerseys is a sign of friendliness and _____. The most well-known jersey swap occurred in 1970. Soccer legends Pele and Bobby Moore swapped jerseys at the _____ of a World Cup match. Since then, soccer stars have needed _____ jerseys because so many players want to swap with them.

end	extra	fairness	helping	tradition	important

★ EXPANDING KNOWLEDGE ★

Shortly after coming to America to play soccer, David Beckham gave a press conference. During the conference, Beckham said that he was happy to play football in the United States. After saying this, he quickly corrected himself and said soccer. Why did Beckham have to do this?

In his home country, the United Kingdom, the sport he plays is called football. In the United States, however, David Beckham's sport is called soccer, and football is the term for an entirely different sport. So where did the word soccer come from? It was part of "Association Football," an old British name for the sport. People informally referred to it as "assoc" before dropping "as" and adding "er" to form "soccer." So while many people think Americans invented the term "soccer," it was actually coined by the British.

1 Why did Beckham correct himself after he said "football" in the press conference?

 a. Football was not played in America.
 b. Football was not that popular in America.
 c. Football and soccer are different sports in his country.
 d. Football in his country has a different name in America.

2 Write T if the statement is true or F if it's not.

 1) Soccer differs from Association Football.
 2) The term "soccer" was first created by the British.

VOCABULARY REVIEW

A Write the correct word next to its definition.

fair	essential	opponent	swap	intense

1 to exchange something with someone: _____

2 treating people in a way that is right or equal: _____

3 a person that you are playing against in sports: _____

4 requiring a lot of effort in a short period of time: _____

B Complete each sentence with a word in the box. (Change the form if needed.)

correct	medical	opposing	refer to	extra	exchange	respect

1 Should I _____ him by any special title or name?

2 I want you to _____ my pronunciation if it is wrong.

3 The player is good enough to make _____ teams nervous.

4 The surgeon should carefully consider the patient's _____ history.

5 The teacher gave the students a(n) _____ week to finish the report.

6 As a sign of _____, he removed his cap before shaking hands with her.

C Find the word that has a similar meaning to the underlined word.

1 We won't <u>supply</u> them with food and water any longer.

   a. share   *b.* provide   *c.* lend   *d.* allow

2 That is an <u>entirely</u> different story from the one I heard before.

   a. partly   *b.* nearly   *c.* totally   *d.* slightly

Before Reading

What do you think are some similarities between humans and animals?

Animal Behavior

As humans, we can be caring and generous, but this is not a quality that sets us apart. Let's take the example of Linda Gustafson's two pets — Toby, a cat, and Katie, a dog. Every evening, Ms. Gustafson would feed Toby and Katie the scraps from her dinner, making sure to put Toby's food high up
5 on the counter away from Katie. But Toby would take pity on Katie when she begged, and he would scoop some food onto the floor so that Katie could eat more. Later in the evening, Katie would leave her cozy spot on the cushion and let Toby sit there, as if _____(A)_____.

But generosity is not limited to domestic animals. Wildlife biologist
10 Kayhan Ostovar observed the same behavior while studying a herd of savannah elephants. ① According to Ostovar, an unknown forest elephant with a badly injured trunk approached one elephant from the savannah herd. ② Cruelty to animals is criticized and opposed by many animal welfare associations. ③ The forest elephant immediately put its trunk in the
15 mouth of the larger elephant to communicate that it couldn't feed itself. ④ Instinctively, the savannah elephant picked up some food and put it in the forest elephant's mouth.

So, why do some animals show such kindness? Scientists think it has something to do with living in a group environment. In a group, animals
20 like elephants rely on each other for food and protection. Thus, they must maintain good relationships with other members of their group. However, animals sometimes help each other even when there is no obvious benefit to be gained. Perhaps they simply enjoy the satisfaction of doing something nice as much as we do.

1 What is the best title for the passage?

    a. Be Kind to Animals

    b. Can Animals Be Nice?

    c. A Way to Communicate with Animals

    d. Humans vs. Animals: Why So Different?

2 Why does the writer mention Toby, a cat, and Katie, a dog?

    a. To show the personality differences in animals

    b. To recommend a good way of feeding animals

    c. To give an example of animals showing kindness

    d. To explain why animals can't get along with each other

3 What is the best choice for blank (A)?

    a. feeling sick

    b. being afraid

    c. searching for food

    d. returning the favor

4 Which sentence is NOT needed in the passage?

    a. ①   *b.* ②   *c.* ③   *d.* ④

5 Why should animals living in a group maintain good relationships with each other?

_____

6 Which example is NOT similar to the ideas presented in the passage?

    a. A fox teaching hunting skills to its baby

    b. An elephant saving a drowning family member

    c. A pack of wolves waiting for an injured group member

    d. A wild chimpanzee handing over food to a hungry man

Fill in the blanks with the correct words.

Human beings can be _____, but so can animals. One example of this can be seen in a dog and cat that live together. The cat shares its food with the dog, and the dog shares its comfortable pillow in _____. This kind of behavior has also been observed in a savannah elephant that fed a(n) _____ forest elephant. Scientists think animals are kind to group members because they may later need a(n) _____. But in some cases it seems as if animals just _____ being nice to one another.

> return   favor   enjoy   caring   injured   benefit

★ EXPANDING KNOWLEDGE ★

Once referred to as the pygmy chimpanzee, the bonobo is now considered more similar to humans than to other primates.

For instance, scientists believe the bonobo is our closest living relative, genetically speaking, for 98% of its DNA is identical to ours. With its slender upper body, shoulders, neck, and long legs, the bonobo more closely resembles a human in appearance than a common chimpanzee does. In fact, it often walks standing on two legs!

Also, the behaviors of the bonobo are similar to ours. When playing in a group, bonobos will laugh and tickle each other. And in experiments, they have demonstrated a capacity for compassion, kindness, patience, and cooperation that is unknown in the animal kingdom beyond humans. They even use tools to accomplish tasks! Isn't it amazing to see ourselves reflected so clearly in an animal?

1 What is the best title for the passage?

  a. The King of the Animal Kingdom
  b. Human Nature Found in Bonobos
  c. Bonobos: Cousins of Chimpanzees
  d. A Comparison of Bonobos and Chimpanzees

2 Write T if the statement is true or F if it's false.

  1) Bonobos are genetically close to humans, sharing 98% of humans' DNA.
  2) Bonobos are social animals that have close relationships with other members.

Unit · 06
VOCABULARY REVIEW

A Write the correct word next to its definition.

satisfaction	primate	compassion	slender	domestic

1 thin in an attractive way: _____

2 relating to an animal that is not wild: _____

3 an animal belonging to the same group as humans and monkeys: _____

4 a strong feeling of sympathy for others that are in a bad situation: _____

B Complete each sentence with a word in the box. (Change the form if needed.)

caring	instinctively	cruelty	tickle	generosity	genetically	take pity on

1 I think it is a bad idea to eat _____ modified foods.

2 He makes a big donation every year. It shows his _____.

3 Laura _____ the old beggar and gave some money to him.

4 Her warm and _____ personality made me fall in love with her.

5 Bob couldn't stop laughing because his sister was _____ his feet.

6 As soon as I heard the explosion, I _____ threw myself to the ground.

C Find the word that has a similar meaning to the underlined word.

1 The Italian restaurant has a very warm and cozy atmosphere.

    a. gloomy   *b.* lively   *c.* romantic   *d.* comfortable

2 Most of the buildings in the city center have an identical shape.

    a. same   *b.* simple   *c.* unique   *d.* artificial

Before Reading
What is the most unique restaurant that you've ever visited?

Special Dining

In a world with almost limitless visual information, sometimes it is important to just close your eyes and take a deep breath. Go ahead and do it right now. Tell me, what do you smell? What do you hear?

5 What do you feel? _____(A)_____, we can strengthen our other senses. This is the idea behind Opaque, the "Dining in the Dark" experience that is sweeping the nation.

Opaque is more than just a restaurant; it is a new way of dining. ① Upon entering Opaque, you will be greeted by our staff in our well-lit lounge area. ② Greeting is a key strategy in the service industry. ③ It is here that you will order your meal and drinks. ④ And remember to leave your coats and bags with our staff. You will not need them in the dark.

Once you are relaxed and ready, you and the other members of your party will be led into the dining room. With your right hand on the shoulder of the person in front of you, you will enter the darkness for a new dining sensation. The members of our wait staff are all visually handicapped people who are trained to help you enjoy your dining experience to the fullest. Without your sense of sight,

20 the simple act of eating will become radically more enjoyable. Smells will become much stronger and flavors much richer.

Critics and guests alike are praising the "Dining in the Dark" experience at Opaque. If you want a dining experience unlike any other, make your reservations today. Join us in the darkness. Join us at Opaque.

1 What is the passage mainly about?

    a. A restaurant reopened after it modernized its equipment.

    b. A restaurant hired blind people to boost their quality of life.

    c. A restaurant uses darkness to create a new dining experience.

    d. A restaurant offers customers tasty food with fresh ingredients.

2 What is the purpose of the passage?

    a. To review a restaurant

    b. To advertise a restaurant

    c. To introduce a new dining culture

    d. To find employees for a new business

3 What is the best choice for blank (A)?

    a. By training our sense of sight

    b. By limiting our sense of touch

    c. By enhancing our body strength

    d. By cutting off our sense of sight

4 Which sentence is NOT needed in the passage?

    a. ①   *b.* ②   *c.* ③   *d.* ④

5 How can customers enter the dining room at Opaque?

_____

6 What is NOT true according to the passage?

    a. You cannot see anything in the dining room.

    b. The entire staff of the restaurant have keen eyesight.

    c. You can taste and smell more in the dark.

    d. Many critics as well as guests like the restaurant.

Fill in the blanks with the correct words.

When we can't see, our other senses become _____. A restaurant called Opaque has used this idea to create a _____ dining experience. Customers enter a well-lit lounge where they place their orders. Then they hold the _____ of a person in front of them and go into the dining room, which is completely dark. There, they are served by a wait staff that is made up of people with _____ handicaps. Eating in the dark makes the food taste _____, and the entire dinner is a special experience.

> visual   richer   unique   stronger   shoulder   sensation

★ EXPANDING KNOWLEDGE ★

I never thought eating could be difficult, but after visiting Opaque I realized how hard it can be. When I received my meal, I couldn't see anything. I could only smell my food. At first I used my knife and fork, but soon I realized that it was easier to eat with my hands. Nobody was able to see me anyway. Meanwhile, all my other senses seemed stronger. For example, I easily heard what people at other tables were talking about.

I even felt like I could taste a single grain of salt. Above all, dining in the dark allowed me to understand how difficult it is to be blind and made me appreciate how lucky I am _____ (A) _____.

1 **What is the best choice for blank (A)?**

   a. to be able to see

   b. to taste delicious food

   c. to dine in a great restaurant

   d. to be able to eat with my hands

2 **Write T if the statement is true or F if it's false.**

   1) The writer had a hard time eating at first.

   2) The writer's ability to see and hear actually improved.

Unit · 07
VOCABULARY REVIEW

A Write the correct word next to its definition.

sweep	praise	limitless	strengthen	relaxed

1 calm and not annoyed or worried: _____

2 to spread quickly through an area: _____

3 to express approval or admiration for someone or something: _____

4 being or appearing to be so abundant that it will never be exhausted: _____

B Complete each sentence with a word in the box. (Change the form if needed.)

critic	strategy	radically	shoulder	handicapped	appreciate	reservation

1 The government has developed a long-term economic _____.

2 I'd _____ it if you let me know the way to the subway station.

3 Ray wants to be an art _____ who writes about rising young artists.

4 I don't want to cancel my _____ that I made eight months in advance.

5 The Internet has _____ changed the way we purchase goods and services.

6 Don't pity physically _____ people. Just treat them the same as everyone else.

C Find the word that has a similar meaning to the underlined word.

1 My favorite chewing gum has a strawberry flavor.

   a. shape   *b.* taste   *c.* smell   *d.* color

2 Everyone greeted Tanya warmly when she came back home after a long absence.

   a. hugged   *b.* accepted   *c.* welcomed   *d.* introduced

Napoleon

Sometimes, a particularly short and aggressive man is said to have a "Napoleon complex." This is based on the idea that the famous French general Napoleon, who conquered much of Europe in the early 19th century, was very short. However, new evidence suggests that Napoleon

5　was not especially short. So, why did this myth about his height develop?

　　One reason had to do with the way people measured height in France and England. (①) Feet and inches were used to measure height in both countries, but the French and English measurements were not the same. (②) So, when Napoleon was described as being 5 feet 2 inches, the English

10　thought this meant he was shorter than average. (③) But this corresponds to 5 feet 6.5 inches in English terms, which means he was actually taller than the average Frenchman! (④)

　　Another reason for the myth about Napoleon's height was his habit of standing beside his bodyguards. His bodyguards were much bigger

15　than normal people, so Napoleon looked short in comparison. Moreover, Napoleon wore a low crown hat, while his bodyguards wore hats with tall crowns. The different hats made Napoleon seem even shorter.

　　Nowadays, many people understand these misconceptions, but Napoleon is still a symbol of short men. Why? It's because his height

20　became such an important part of British culture from the early 1800s, when Britain and France were enemies. The British often made fun of Napoleon as a way of _____(A)_____ the French, so jokes about Napoleon's height became very popular. That's why the myth that he was a short man is still around today.

1 What is the best title for the passage?

a. The Truth about Napoleon's Height

b. The Theory of the Napoleon Complex

c. British People's Attitude about Napoleon

d. How Napoleon Overcame His Physical Disadvantage

2 What can be inferred from the 1st paragraph?

a. Napoleon was the shortest conqueror of Europe.

b. People who are short and aggressive admire Napoleon.

c. Napoleon was the exception of a famous myth about height.

d. People believe Napoleon tried to make up for his height by being aggressive.

3 Where would the following sentence best fit?

In France, an inch was 2.71 cm, whereas in England, an inch was just 2.41 cm.

a. ①   b. ②   c. ③   d. ④

4 Why did standing next to his bodyguards make Napoleon look short?

5 What is the best choice for blank (A)?

a. fighting off

b. looking up to

c. looking down on

d. making peace with

6 Write T if the statement is true or F if it's false.

1) Napoleon was not shorter than the average Frenchman.

2) The British used to make fun of Napoleon's hat.

Fill in the blanks with the correct words.

_____ about Napoleon's Height

Reasons
- The French inch and the British inch had _____ measurements.
- Napoleon often stood beside his _____ bodyguards.
- Napoleon's hat was _____ than his bodyguards' hats.

Why the myth exists today
- Napoleon's short height was established in British culture, due to Britain's _____ with France.

rivalry   different   misconceptions   shorter   large   average

★ EXPANDING KNOWLEDGE ★

In 1804, Napoleon introduced the Napoleonic Code, also known as the Civil Code. The Napoleonic Code created a unified, logical system of law across all of Europe.

Most of the new laws were helpful, but not everybody benefited from them. The Code limited many freedoms of women. For instance, women could not buy or sell property without their husband's permission. The Code also strengthened divorce laws and made husbands the rulers of their homes. _____(A)_____, the Code was in many ways progressive. It resulted in a system of public works that created canals, harbors, and improved roads throughout the continent. The educational system also benefited, which resulted in the creation of private schools and an increased emphasis on literacy.

Still influential to this day, the Napoleonic Code remains the largest legacy of Napoleon.

1 What is the best choice for blank (A)?

  a. Therefore   b. As a result   c. In the same way   d. On the other hand

2 Write T if the statement is true or F if it's false.

  1) The Napoleonic Code weakened husbands' power at home.
  2) More people could be educated under the Napoleonic Code.

Unit · 08
VOCABULARY REVIEW

A Write the correct word next to its definition.

aggressive	logical	myth	permission	emphasis

1 seeming sensible or reasonable: _____

2 a story or idea that is believed but not true: _____

3 behaving in an angry, violent way as if ready to attack: _____

4 the act of allowing someone to do something officially: _____

B Complete each sentence with a word in the box. (Change the form if needed.)

unified	literacy	strengthen	average	misconception	introduce	measure

1 The lawmakers will _____ a bill to ban text message spam.

2 People think that pigs are dirty, but that is a common _____.

3 _____ rates are rising due to the improved education system.

4 Their final goal is to form a(n) _____ government in their country.

5 I was disappointed because my performance on the test was below _____.

6 The government plans to _____ the welfare system to help people in need.

C Find the word that has a similar meaning to the underlined word.

1 The progressive education system was not welcomed by most people.

   a. latest   *b.* old-fashioned   *c.* innovative   *d.* organized

2 He was an influential politician in the 1980s.

   a. loved   *b.* unpopular   *c.* honest   *d.* powerful

★Unit★
09 LITERATURE

Before Reading
Have you ever felt like you were in Wonderland?

Alice's Adventures in Wonderland

Alice was sitting by the river with her sister and feeling terribly bored.
Her sister was reading a book, but Alice had nothing to do. She
was thinking about picking some wildflowers when she saw a
white rabbit run by. It wasn't strange to see a rabbit. There

5 were many rabbits living near the river. But this rabbit
seemed to be talking to itself! Over and over again, it
was saying, "Oh dear! I shall be late!" Then the rabbit
stopped and looked at its watch, before hurrying on.

Now this sight was very strange. Alice had never seen a rabbit wearing

10 a watch before. Curious, she stood up and began to follow the rabbit.
She chased it across a field and watched as it jumped down a large hole.
Without hesitating, Alice followed the rabbit down the hole. If she had
stopped to think, she might have wondered how she would get back out.
But instead, she jumped right in and began to fall.

15 Either the hole was very _____(A)_____ or Alice was falling very
_____(B)_____. She had a lot of time to wonder what would happen next.
She tried looking down, but it was too dark to see anything. "I wonder how
deep I've fallen," she thought. It seemed like miles down, down, down. It
seemed like the fall would never end! "I must be getting near the center of

20 the earth," she thought. "I wonder if I shall fall right through the earth! How
funny it'll seem to come out among the people that walk with their heads
downward!" And then, suddenly, she landed with a thump in a pile of dry
leaves. Her fall was finally over!

1 What is the best title for the passage?

    a. Alice Finds a Large Rabbit Hole

    b. Alice Falls Down the Rabbit Hole

    c. Alice Meets a Rabbit in Her Dream

    d. Alice and a Rabbit Become Friends

2 Why did Alice think the white rabbit she saw was strange?

_____

3 What can be inferred from the underlined sentence?

    a. Alice wasn't used to jumping from heights.

    b. Alice knew how to get back out of the hole.

    c. Alice tended to be very careful in everything she did.

    d. Alice was careless about what might happen to her afterwards.

4 What is the best pair for blanks (A) and (B)?

	(A)		(B)
a.	deep	—	slowly
b.	large	—	fast
c.	dark	—	fast
d.	small	—	slowly

5 How did Alice's feelings change throughout the story?

    a. bored → afraid

    b. bored → curious

    c. excited → curious

    d. afraid → excited

6 Write T if the statement is true or F if it's false.

    1) Alice and her sister were chasing a white rabbit near the river.

    2) Alice regretted following the rabbit when she was falling down the hole.

Fill in the blanks with the correct words.

Alice was _____ and sitting by the river when a white rabbit ran past. At first, the rabbit seemed _____. But then it looked at a watch and talked to itself, worrying that it would be late. Alice grew _____ and decided to follow the rabbit. The rabbit ran through a field and then jumped into a large hole. Without thinking, Alice jumped into the hole, too. Her fall _____ for a long time. She seemed to fall for miles. Then finally, she _____ on a pile of leaves.

landed	curious	lasted	bored	ordinary	fallen

★ EXPANDING KNOWLEDGE ★

Lewis Carroll's *Alice's Adventures in Wonderland* is about a girl named Alice who falls down a rabbit hole and finds herself in a fantasy land filled with unusual, imaginary creatures. Although the story sounds like pure fiction, it was actually inspired by real life.

In 1856, Carroll became friends with three sisters named Lorina, Alice, and Edith. Over the next few years, he spent a lot of time with the girls and made up stories to entertain them. One was about a girl named Alice and the fantastic adventures she had underground. Lorina and Edith appeared in the story as well. Alice loved the story so much that she asked Carroll to write it down. Before publishing the script, Carroll had illustrator John Tenniel draw pictures for the book.

Alice's Adventures in Wonderland was an instant success. Today it has been translated into 125 languages and remains a favorite tale among children and adults alike.

1 What is the passage mainly about?

a. How a story was created
b. The characters in a novel
c. The main plot of a novel
d. Why a story is loved by everyone

2 What is NOT true about *Alice's Adventures in Wonderland*?

a. It is based on the story that Carroll told his daughters.
b. Some real people appear in the story.
c. It was illustrated by John Tenniel.
d. It became very popular as soon as it was published.

VOCABULARY REVIEW

A Write the correct word next to its definition.

translate	instant	script	hesitate	illustrator

1 to change text into another language: _____

2 someone who draws pictures for books: _____

3 happening or produced immediately without delay: _____

4 to be slow to do something because you are not sure: _____

B Complete each sentence with a word in the box. (Change the form if needed.)

fiction	inspire	curious	downward	terribly	creature	underground

1 After we finished the marathon, we felt _____ thirsty.

2 The writer composed a poem _____ by the beauty of nature.

3 Although the story of the movie seems very real, it is just _____.

4 Many people are _____ about the reason why she left so suddenly.

5 Some animals, like moles and earthworms, spend their entire lives _____.

6 He insisted he saw a(n) _____ from outer space, but no one believed him.

C Find the word that has a similar meaning to the underlined word.

1 The child sang the same song <u>over and over again</u>.

    a. loudly   *b.* regularly   *c.* slowly   *d.* repeatedly

2 The dog <u>chased</u> the sheep but couldn't catch it.

    a. looked after   *b.* ran after   *c.* growled at   *d.* ran from

Before Reading
How is your handwriting? Is it neat or messy?

Handwriting

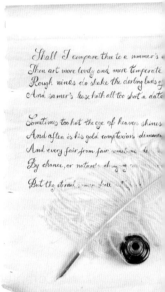

What, besides our fingerprints, distinguishes us as individuals? You may be surprised to learn that our handwriting does. Everyone has a unique handwriting style that reflects his or her personality. The great Chinese philosopher <u>Confucius</u> made
5   this point when he said: "Beware of a man whose handwriting sways like reeds in the wind."

You can discover a lot about a person's character just by examining his or her writing. For example, people with neat handwriting are usually reliable, while those with messy writing
10   may be secretive. Small letters mean the person might be shy, _____(A)_____ big letters indicate the person likes attention. Handwriting analysts also look for linking. If the letters are joined, the person is probably cautious, but if there are spaces between the letters, the person might be artistic.

15   Handwriting analysis has many practical uses. For example, the police sometimes employ handwriting analysts to compare a suspect's normal writing with a forged document. The analysts look for major differences between the two samples to determine whether the suspect committed the crime. Many companies also employ handwriting analysts when making
20   hiring decisions. Analysts check the handwriting of job applicants to find out more about their personal qualities. Some even say handwriting analysis can be used to change a person's bad habits and traits through a process known as handwriting therapy.

However, it is important to realize that handwriting analysis
25   has limitations. Analysts cannot tell a person's age, race, gender, or even whether he or she is left- or right-handed. _____(B)_____, handwriting can reveal interesting information about people in many situations. So the next time you see someone's handwriting, guess what the person's personality is like.

1 What is the passage mainly about?

    a. Different styles of handwriting

    b. How to improve your handwriting

    c. The history of handwriting analysis

    d. What handwriting reveals about people

2 Why does the writer quote <u>Confucius</u>?

    a. To explain the origin of handwriting analysis

    b. To show how great the philosophy of Confucius was

    c. To introduce a common misunderstanding about handwriting

    d. To emphasize the relationship between handwriting and personality

3 What can we guess about a person whose handwriting features small letters?

_____

4 What is the best pair for blanks (A) and (B)?

	(A)		(B)
a.	as if	—	Therefore
b.	as if	—	Moreover
c.	whereas	—	Nevertheless
d.	whereas	—	Consequently

5 What is NOT a situation in which handwriting analysis can be used?

    a. Investigating a crime

    b. Hiring employees

    c. Correcting bad habits

    d. Identifying a person's race

6 Write T if the statement is true or F if it's false.

    1) If a person's letters don't touch each other, he or she might have artistic talent.

    2) We can discover if a person is left-handed or right-handed through handwriting analysis.

Fill in the blanks with the correct words.

Handwriting Analysis

Indicating _____	• Neat handwriting: reliability • Messy handwriting: secretiveness • Small letters: _____ • Spaces between letters: an artistic nature
_____ uses	• Used to determine forgery • Used by _____ to learn more about their potential employees • Can be used to correct a person's bad qualities through handwriting _____

shyness   practical   therapy   personality   companies   habits

★ EXPANDING KNOWLEDGE ★

According to graphotherapy, people can improve their personalities through manual changes in their handwriting. But how is it possible? When you write, it involves a series of movements using rhythm, speed, pressure, and direction. These movements are influenced by your deepest feelings and emotions. Therefore, handwriting _____(A)_____ our physical, mental, and emotional states. This explains why each person has a unique way of writing, even though everybody learns how to write based on an established pattern. In fact, one scientist calculated that the possibility of two people having the exact same handwriting is one in 68 trillion.

Graphotherapy is said to work best with children because they're still developing their writing style and personality. However, it may be possible to see positive changes in even the most stubborn adults.

1 What is the best choice for blank (A)?

a. alters   *b.* reflects   *c.* controls   *d.* ignores

2 Write T if the statement is true or F if it's false.

1) There is little chance that the handwriting of two different people is identical.

2) Children's handwriting is more difficult to change than adults'.

Unit ⋆ 10
VOCABULARY REVIEW

A Write the correct word next to its definition.

manual	forge	fingerprint	sway	suspect

1 to move slowly from side to side: _____

2 relating to the use of your hands: _____

3 to make an illegal copy of something: _____

4 a person believed to have committed a crime: _____

B Complete each sentence with a word in the box. (Change the form if needed.)

analyst	reveal	trait	beware of	stubborn	applicant	messy

1 You should _____ making hasty decisions.

2 Selfishness is a very unattractive personality _____.

3 She was chosen for the job from over 1,000 _____.

4 The man would not _____ the secret to his success.

5 She is too _____ to change her mind about anything.

6 My room is so _____ that I need to clean it up right away.

C Find the word that has a similar meaning to the underlined word.

1 The study <u>indicates</u> a link between stress and cancer.

    a. breaks   *b.* shows   *c.* agrees   *d.* builds

2 Be <u>cautious</u> about giving out personal information.

    a. careful   *b.* nervous   *c.* positive   *d.* honest

Before Reading
Why do so many goods have prices ending in the number nine?

Odd Pricing

We often pay $9.99 for a product rather than $10. Why do so many prices end in odd numbers such as 99? There are a few theories.

The most well-known theory involves the *Chicago Daily News*. In the 1870s, its owner, Melville E. Stone, decided that what Chicago needed was a penny newspaper to compete with the nickel papers that were available at the time. But there was a problem: with most goods priced at even figures for the convenience of shoppers, there weren't many pennies to spare. To get more pennies into circulation, he persuaded store owners to reduce

15 their prices slightly. He said that buyers would be more likely to purchase a product if it cost "only" $0.99 rather than $1, and he was correct. Soon more pennies were available for people to buy the *Daily News*, and the newspaper's circulation increased.

However, there is a more likely explanation for today's custom of

20 having nearly every price end in odd numbers. (①) In the 1880s, a period of economic boom, the American retail market experienced a high degree of competition. (②) To compete with their larger rivals, smaller companies in Chicago began to use "just under" pricing. (③) Such a pricing strategy had a powerful psychological effect on

25 customers, making the products appear cheaper. (④)

From its origins in the small businesses of Chicago, the practice of pricing goods at odd numbers has evolved to become a common tactic around the world. Whatever you're interested in purchasing, wherever you

30 are in the world, the psychological trick of odd pricing will probably be used to persuade you to buy.

1 What is the best title for the passage?

a. Pricing Strategies in Marketing
b. The Origin of a Pricing Strategy
c. The Impact of Competition on Retail Prices
d. America's Economic Situation in the 19th Century

2 Why did Stone persuade shop owners to lower prices?

a. To get rid of goods in stock
b. To make more pennies available
c. To strengthen their competitiveness
d. To get over the poor economic situation

3 Where would the following sentence best fit?

> For example, they advertised products that their competitors sold for $2 at $1.99.

a. ①   b. ②   c. ③   d. ④

4 In the late 19th century, small companies in Chicago adopted a new pricing strategy in order to _____.

5 Odd pricing is a marketing trick that gives buyers _____.

a. various options for payment
b. the illusion that prices are low
c. the expectation of high quality
d. a discount on volume purchases

6 Write T if the statement is true or F if it's false.

1) Odd pricing is setting a price at a little more than an even dollar amount.
2) Odd pricing is a strategy limited to a particular sector of industry.

Fill in the blanks with the correct words.

Did you ever wonder why product prices often _____ in 99?
One theory is that it was started by a newspaper publisher in the 1870s.
While most papers in those days cost a nickel, his only cost a penny. But
he was _____ that consumers didn't have many pennies. So
he convinced stores to _____ their prices by one cent. Another
theory is that smaller businesses started lowering their prices slightly in
order to _____ with larger businesses. Either way, the practice of
"_____ pricing" is now used all around the world.

| compete | end | lower | odd | worried | figures |

★ EXPANDING KNOWLEDGE ★

Price is more than just a number. It can have a strong
_____(A)_____ effect on shoppers. For example,
a high price can make you believe that a product is
of a high quality, even if it isn't. Also, prices that end
in odd numbers, such as $9.99, create an impression
that a product is a good deal, even though $9.99
is just one cent less than $10. This technique is
particularly powerful when prices of goods are grouped into ranges, such as $100 –
$199. In this case, a product priced $199 would appear in a lower price range than a
product costing $200. This makes the product seem even cheaper. So, if you want to
become a smart consumer, think carefully about the price of a product or service before
making a purchase. The price may not be as good as it seems.

1 What is the best choice for blank (A)?

a. visual
b. behavioral
c. economical
d. psychological

2 What is NOT true according to the passage?

a. Consumers tend to associate high prices with high quality.
b. A price ending in odd numbers is viewed as a better price.
c. Price endings are used to keep items within a higher price range.
d. A price may not be as much of a bargain as it seems.

A Write the correct word next to its definition.

evolve	available	retail	theory	psychological

1 relating to your mind or feelings: _____

2 to develop and change over a long period of time: _____

3 an idea that explains how and why something happens: _____

4 related to the sale of goods in small quantities to consumers: _____

B Complete each sentence with a word in the box. (Change the form if needed.)

slightly	persuade	boom	odd	deal	impression	competition

1 His speech made a deep _____ on the audience.

2 The two students' answers were only _____ different.

3 There is a lot of _____ between mobile phone companies.

4 I got a really good _____ on my new bike and saved money.

5 No matter how much you try to _____ her, she won't give in.

6 The economic _____ of the 1950s raised the standard of living.

C Find the word that has a similar meaning to the underlined word.

1 Tickets must be <u>purchased</u> in advance.

    a. sold   *b.* bought   *c.* invested   *d.* reserved

2 The dictionary explains the <u>origin</u> of words.

    a. meaning   *b.* use   *c.* beginning   *d.* change

Art Preservation

Rodin's *The Thinker*, Michelangelo's painting on the ceiling of the Sistine Chapel, Angkor Wat in Cambodia, and thousands of other ancient pieces of art and architecture continue to amaze people today. These great works have survived for many centuries because people have made great efforts to preserve them. However, not everyone agrees on the best form of preservation. Some people advocate art "restoration" and others prefer art "conservation." So, what are the differences between these two approaches?

Restorers clean, repair, and sometimes rebuild artwork. Most restorers have some artistic training, and they learn how to do their craft

15 through trial and error. Their aim is to return artwork to its former glory, making it look like it did when it was first created. For example, restorers may retouch the colors on a painting or replace broken or worn parts of a statue.

Art conservators, _____(A)_____, are committed to simply keeping

20 ancient artwork in the best possible condition. Usually highly trained professionals, conservators take a scientific approach to their task. They touch the artwork as little as possible and ensure that the conditions are perfect to prevent further damage and wear.

However, conservation and restoration also have much in common.

25 Most importantly, the primary goal of both conservators and restorers is to maintain a work of art's original features. Conservators do this by keeping the original parts of the artwork in good condition. Likewise, restorers are also concerned with providing an accurate representation of artwork in its original form. If they cannot find reliable historical evidence of what the

30 artwork originally looked like, they won't do any restoration work on it at all.

1 What is the passage mainly about?

    a. The difficulties of preserving art

    b. Two different ways of preserving art

    c. The development of art preservation techniques

    d. Controversies over the best way of preserving art

2 What are art restorers most UNLIKELY to do?

    a. To remove dust from paintings

    b. To repair broken parts of sculptures

    c. To make a piece of art better than the original

    d. To fill areas of a portrait where paint has fallen off

3 What is the best choice for blank (A)?

    a. in fact   *b.* after all

    c. therefore   *d.* on the other hand

4 What is NOT true about art conservators?

    a. They use skills learned by experience.

    b. They make sure artwork is in good condition.

    c. They try to protect artwork from being damaged.

    d. They perform a minimal amount of maintenance on artwork.

5 Both art restorers and art conservators consider it most important to

_____ .

6 Write T if the statement is true or F if it's false.

    1) Conservators handle artwork in a scientific way.

    2) Restorers use their imagination when they are unsure of the original appearance of an art piece.

STRATEGIC ORGANIZER

Fill in the blanks with the correct words.

Ways to Preserve Art

Art restoration
- To preserve art by 1) _____ it
- To make art look the same as when it was originally made
- How: 2) _____, rebuild, and clean art

Art conservation
- To protect art without making any 3) _____
- To keep artwork in good condition
- How: 4) _____ ideal conditions

Common goal: to preserve the 5) _____ features of artwork

> wear   changes   maintain   original   repair   restoring

★ EXPANDING KNOWLEDGE ★

The most recent restoration of da Vinci's *Last Supper* was completed in May 1999. The first and foremost task was to prevent further deterioration of the painting. A chemical analysis showed that paint from earlier restorations was eating away at da Vinci's original paint. Restorers decided to remove all the paint that had been added to the piece after it was originally finished. Such a difficult task required great attention to detail. Several sophisticated techniques were used, including radar and lasers. Consequently, the restoration was a slow and difficult process. An area that was no bigger than a postage stamp could be restored in several stages. Ultimately, the twenty years of hard work paid off. The painting was restored while keeping its original look intact. Today, the painting is preserved by a sophisticated air filtration system. Groups of no more than 25 people are allowed to see the painting for just 15 minutes at a time.

1 What does the underlined sentence mean?

a. There was a shortage of professionals.
b. The damage to the painting was severe.
c. The technique they used was not appropriate.
d. The work was highly sophisticated and difficult.

2 Write T if the statement is true or F if it's false.

1) The recent restoration of da Vinci's *Last Supper* included uncovering layers of paint.
2) *Last Supper* is not open to the public because of the restoration process.

VOCABULARY REVIEW

A Write the correct word next to its definition.

| intact | primary | advocate | former | preserve |

1 to publicly support something: _____

2 not harmed, broken, or damaged: _____

3 main, most important or first in order: _____

4 to protect something from being destroyed: _____

B Complete each sentence with a word in the box. (Change the form if needed.)

| rebuild | deterioration | original | pay off | artistic | restoration | sophisticated |

1 The painter discovered his _____ talent at an early age.

2 Water damage to the building has caused serious _____.

3 One year after the earthquake, the buildings were _____.

4 It'll take a long time, but I'm sure their efforts will _____ someday.

5 The _____ of the old palace is expected to take at least three years.

6 The differences are minute and can only be detected with _____ equipment.

C Find the word that has a similar meaning to the underlined word.

1 I've heard from a <u>reliable</u> source that they are engaged.

   a. wrong   b. different   c. interesting   d. dependable

2 She <u>amazed</u> us by winning first prize in the speech contest.

   a. terrified   b. pleased   c. surprised   d. disappointed

Supertaster

Do you hate the taste of broccoli, cabbage, coffee, or even dark chocolate? Then you might be a "supertaster," someone whose sense of taste is very strong. Supertasters are particularly sensitive to bitterness, which is why they often dislike cabbage and coffee.

When it comes to taste, there are three main groups of people. Around 50 percent of the population are medium-tasters, with a normal range of sensitivity to different tastes. 25 percent are non-
10 tasters who have a poor sense of taste. And the remaining 25 percent of people are supertasters. Supertasters have more taste buds than others, and their taste buds are more sensitive to the bitterness of a specific chemical substance found in many foods. Evidence suggests that a high percentage of Africans, Asians, and South Americans are supertasters, and that women
15 are more likely to be supertasters than men.

Why are some people supertasters? One theory is that this gene has evolved to keep people safe from poisonous substances. Supertasters are better able to distinguish dangerous plants by taste. _____(A)_____, being a supertaster might also be an evolutionary disadvantage, since they have a
20 more limited diet than medium-tasters and non-tasters. Also, it was thought that supertasters might be healthier since supertasters dislike overly fatty and sugary foods. But new research shows that most supertasters enjoy highly salted food, as a high salt content disguises bitterness.

All in all, then, being a supertaster is a mixed blessing. Supertasters
25 suffer less from obesity, but their salty diet has a negative effect on their health. To overcome this, they need more creativity in cooking and strong willpower in their food choices.

1 What is the best title for the passage?

a. The Hard Life of Supertasters

b. What Makes Some People Supertasters

c. Supertasters' Concerns about Their Health

d. Why Supertasters Can't Taste Food Normally

2 What can be inferred from the 2nd paragraph?

a. Supertasters are likely to have a bigger tongue.

b. Supertasters are hardly found in some countries.

c. Supertasters are more prevalent among certain races.

d. Supertasters can't detect any taste other than bitterness.

3 What is the best choice for blank (A)?

a. Therefore

b. However

c. In addition

d. As a result

4 Why do supertasters like salty food?

_____

5 What does the underlined part mean?

a. Being a supertaster is a good thing.

b. Being a supertaster has negative health effects.

c. Being a supertaster has both good and bad points.

d. Being a supertaster has more advantages than disadvantages.

6 What is NOT true about supertasters?

a. They have more taste buds.

b. They avoid sugary and fatty foods.

c. They enjoy a wider range of foods than others.

d. They should be careful about their diet.

Fill in the blanks with the correct words.

Supertasters are people with an exceptionally _____ sense of taste. They often dislike _____ things, like cabbage and coffee. About 25 percent of the population are supertasters. Many of these people are African, Asian, or South American, and the _____ of them are women. A theory says that supertasters developed their sensitivity to help them avoid eating _____ plants. Supertasters usually dislike fatty and sugary foods, which is good for their health. However, they tend to eat too much _____ food. Therefore, being a supertaster has both good and bad points.

sensitive	salty	bitter	majority	evolve	poisonous

★ EXPANDING KNOWLEDGE ★

Do you wonder if you are a supertaster? Here is an easy test you can do to find out what kind of taster you are. This test allows you to count the number of taste buds you have. To do this, you will need some blue food coloring, a piece of paper with a 7 mm-wide hole in it, and a magnifying glass. Put the blue food coloring on the tip of your tongue. Your tongue will turn blue, but the area where your taste buds are will stay pink. Put the paper on your tongue and use the magnifying glass to count the number of pink dots in the hole. If there are fewer than 15, you are a non-taster. If you have between 15 and 35, you are a medium-taster. Having more than 35 means you are a supertaster!

1 **What is the passage mainly about?**

a. The function of taste buds

b. The way to find taste buds

c. The way to identify a supertaster

d. A food that appeases supertasters

2 **What is NOT mentioned as a tool for taking the supertaster test?**

a. blue food coloring

b. a piece of paper with a hole

c. a cup of water

d. a magnifying glass

Unit ★ 13
VOCABULARY REVIEW

A Write the correct word next to its definition.

limited	willpower	disguise	distinguish	poisonous

1 very harmful; causing death or illness: _____

2 the ability to control your mind and behavior: _____

3 to recognize the difference between two people or things: _____

4 to change or hide something so that people do not notice it: _____

B Complete each sentence with a word in the box. (Change the form if needed.)

tongue	chemical	blessing	fatty	sensitive	highly	bitterness

1 Having good friends is a real _____ .

2 You'd better avoid _____ foods if you want to lose weight.

3 Don't stick your _____ out because it is very rude behavior.

4 I should put on sunscreen because my skin is _____ to sunlight.

5 This _____ substance is toxic, so it must be kept away from children.

6 I'd like to hire Mark because he is a _____ skilled computer programmer.

C Find the word that has a similar meaning to the underlined word.

1 Are there any fashion magazines that you <u>particularly</u> like?

    a. rarely   *b.* overly   *c.* especially   *d.* accidentally

2 Our biggest <u>disadvantage</u> is that we don't have anyone who can speak Chinese.

    a. goal   *b.* handicap   *c.* necessity   *d.* shortage

Before Reading
Who do you think was the greatest scientist in history?

Great Inventors

Two of the greatest minds of the early modern age were Nikola Tesla and Thomas Edison. However, schoolchildren today only learn about the great accomplishments of Edison. Rarely are they taught about Tesla. So how can his scientific contributions be considered comparable to Edison's?

5   Tesla was a skilled scientist and inventor. Shortly after coming to America from Serbia in 1884, he began working with Edison on many important projects. Edison had just invented the electric light bulb and needed a system to distribute electricity. Thus, he created the direct current (DC) electricity system, which he marketed as a safe and effective electricity

10 technology. But, Tesla understood that DC had serious drawbacks and knew that the system would not be able to generate and deliver electricity across a large grid. Therefore, he developed the alternating current (AC) system, a direct competitor to the DC system. Following this, Tesla left Edison and the two great scientists became lifelong rivals.

15 In the end, Tesla's AC system won out, and today it is used in millions of homes. Edison's light bulb was a brilliant invention, but it would have been of little value without a practical and reliable way to deliver electricity. _____(A)_____ Tesla's AC system, Edison's light bulb became an essential part of modern life. _____(B)_____ this fact, Tesla remains virtually

20 unknown.

To understand why, we have to consider Edison's business skills. Edison was a brilliant self-promoter who was able to sell both his products and himself. Tesla, on the other hand, lacked the business sense needed to market his

25 inventions as commercial products. However, his contributions to science are just as important as those of Edison, even though few remember the work of Nikola Tesla.

1 What is the best title for the passage?

    a. Great Inventions in Modern Life

    b. The Age of Multi-Talented People

    c. Nikola Tesla: The Forgotten Genius

    d. Thomas Edison: Father of Electricity

2 How does the writer introduce the topic?

    a. By criticizing the education system

    b. By explaining how electricity works

    c. By comparing two important figures

    d. By correcting a common misconception

3 What was Tesla's understanding about Edison's DC system? (Choose two.)

    a. It was a seriously defective system.

    b. It was a safe way to generate electricity.

    c. Electricity couldn't travel long distances with it.

    d. It was necessary to commercialize the light bulb.

4 What is the best pair for blanks (A) and (B)?

          (A)   (B)

    a. In spite of — With

    b. With   — Without

    c. Without   — Because of

    d. Thanks to — In spite of

5 Why is Tesla unknown while Edison is still so famous?

6 What is true about Nikola Tesla?

    a. He helped Edison invent the electric light bulb.

    b. He supported Edison's DC electricity system.

    c. He maintained a good partnership with Edison.

    d. His electricity system is widely used today.

STRATEGIC SUMMARY

Fill in the blanks with the correct words.

Nikola Tesla and Thomas Edison were both great inventors. However, these days, Edison remains famous while Tesla has been largely _____. When Tesla first immigrated to America, he worked with Edison. Edison had just _____ the light bulb and he developed the direct current system to _____ electricity to homes. Tesla thought it was a(n) _____ method, so he created the alternating current system. The two became rivals, but Tesla's system is still used today. However, few remember Tesla's work because he lacked the business skills to _____ his inventions, which Edison was better at doing.

> inefficient   scientist   forgotten   promote   deliver   invented

★ EXPANDING KNOWLEDGE ★

In the late 19th century, a war of currents was being fought. On one side was Thomas Edison with his DC system. On the other were George Westinghouse and Nikola Tesla with their AC system. The turning point occurred at Niagara Falls. George Westinghouse won the contract to generate electricity at the falls using Tesla's AC system. But many doubted that AC could generate enough power for the nearby city of Buffalo, New York. Tesla, on the other hand, was sure the system could generate enough power for not only Buffalo, but also the entire Eastern Seaboard. Finally, on November 16, 1896, Tesla proved the skeptics wrong by generating power at Niagara Falls and sending it to Buffalo. Tesla's AC generators had worked! Niagara Falls proved the _____(A)_____ of Tesla's AC system, and by the early 20th century direct current had become just a memory in the history of the mass generation of electricity.

1 What is the best choice for blank (A)?

  a. source   b. popularity   c. superiority   d. limitations

2 What is NOT true according to the passage?

  a. Tesla was confident of the success of the AC system.
  b. Tesla won in the war of currents as everybody had expected.
  c. It was possible to send electricity over a distance with the AC system.
  d. Niagara Falls played an important role in the acceptance of AC.

VOCABULARY REVIEW

A Write the correct word next to its definition.

contract	reliable	lack	skeptic	brilliant

1 very clever and skillful: _____

2 to have not enough of something that is needed: _____

3 a person who doubts the truth or value of an idea: _____

4 an official agreement between two or more people: _____

B Complete each sentence with a word in the box. (Change the form if needed.)

skilled	lifelong	market	distribute	in the end	turning point	generate

1 Solar cells _____ electricity by capturing sunlight.

2 I tried for a year to change her mind but gave up _____ .

3 His _____ dream of becoming a movie star had finally come true.

4 The trip was a(n) _____ in my life and everything changed after that.

5 She is a(n) _____ writer who knows how to make her stories interesting.

6 In order to _____ a product well, you need to understand public demand.

C Find the word that has a similar meaning to the underlined word.

1 The stain on my shirt has <u>virtually</u> disappeared.

　　a. never　　　　*b.* finally　　　　*c.* perfectly　　　　*d.* practically

2 The technology is very useful, but it still has some <u>drawbacks</u>.

　　a. benefits　　　　*b.* weaknesses　　　　*c.* functions　　　　*d.* popularity

An Interview with a Criminal Profiler

Criminal profilers are people who investigate crimes, and they have become very popular in movies and TV dramas these days. The following is an interview with a criminal profiler.

Q: _____(A)_____

A: Criminal profiling is basically trying to get inside the mind of a criminal. Based on the evidence, we try to work out how they think and what sort of person they are. This allows police to narrow down the possible suspects in a case. It also helps them to
10 predict what the criminal might do next.

Q: _____(B)_____

A: Sure. James A. Brussel famously helped detectives in the "Mad Bomber" case. Between 1940 and 1956, a serial bomber was terrorizing New York. Using evidence from the crime scenes and from letters left behind
15 by the "Mad Bomber," Brussel built up a profile of the criminal. He told police to look for an overweight, single, Roman Catholic, male mechanic from Connecticut who used to work for an energy company. Sure enough, a few weeks later the police found the Mad Bomber, George Metersky, and he fit all of these characteristics. Even the clothes he wore
20 matched Brussel's prediction!

Q: _____(C)_____

A: Yes, it is. Shows like *Criminal Minds* make it seem like we are responsible for identifying and catching criminals all by ourselves. But, in reality, there are _____(D)_____ to profiling. We usually can't identify the criminal.
25 All we can do is identify the type of person the criminal is, and there may be 10 or more suspects who fit that particular personality type. So, our role is really to help police with their normal detective work.

64

1 What is the interview mainly about?

  a. The work that criminal profilers do
  b. The difficulties that criminal profilers face
  c. The fantasy that people have about criminal profilers
  d. The cooperation between criminal profilers and police

2 Match the question to each blank.

  1) (A)•   • a. Do you think your job is romanticized on TV?
  2) (B)•   • b. What is criminal profiling?
  3) (C)•   • c. Have there been any cases where criminal profiling played
                       an important role?

3 Criminal profilers help police to _____
and to _____ .

4 What is NOT mentioned in the example of James A. Brussel?

  a. The police couldn't catch the criminal for over 10 years.
  b. Brussel had investigated crimes with the police for several years.
  c. Crime scene evidence was used to predict the characteristics of the criminal.
  d. Brussel even correctly predicted the criminal's clothing style.

5 What is the best choice for blank (D)?

  a. priorities   *b.* limitations
  c. advantages   *d.* prohibitions

6 What is NOT true about criminal profiling?

  a. It is a great topic for movies and dramas.
  b. It is one of the tools used to find criminals.
  c. It is a job that can easily be misunderstood.
  d. It can identify a criminal on the spot.

Fill in the blanks with the correct words.

Criminal Profiling	— Understanding a criminal's _____

How it helps
- Narrows down the suspects and _____ the criminal's next move

A famous case of criminal profiling: The "Mad Bomber" case
- Using _____ from evidence at the crime scenes
- Identifying _____ characteristics of the bomber

Limitation of criminal profiling
- Only identifying the _____ of person that a criminal is

specific	clues	mind	type	predicts	reality

★ EXPANDING KNOWLEDGE ★

What can you do with fingerprints, DNA, and blood? Why, solve a crime, of course! _____(A)_____ is called forensics. Forensic scientists help police link suspects to crime scenes. Their work involves everything from studying human bodies to tracking weather patterns. Sometimes they carry out detailed examinations of bodies to determine the exact cause of death. At other times, they look for evidence of drugs or explosives. They can even study bones to figure out people's age at the time of death. They can also use saliva left on a chewed pencil or DNA from flakes of skin to identify a murderer. Thanks to the work of forensic scientists, solving crimes has become much easier.

1 What is the best choice for blank (A)?

   a. Using science to solve crimes
   b. Inspecting dead bodies to help police
   c. Studying human nature to decrease crimes
   d. Analyzing the process of committing a crime

2 Write T if the statement is true or F if it's false.

   1) Forensic scientists' work is to study the causes of crimes to prevent them.
   2) Forensic scientists can find out how and when a person died.

VOCABULARY REVIEW

A Write the correct word next to its definition.

investigate	terrorize	romanticize	fit	predict

1 to say that something will happen in the future: _____

2 to look carefully at facts in order to find the truth: _____

3 to agree with, match, or be suitable for something: _____

4 to describe or regard others as better than they really are: _____

B Complete each sentence with a word in the box. (Change the form if needed.)

profile	work out	criminal	evidence	by oneself	limitation	narrow down

1 They will _____ the list to three candidates.

2 So far, I have done it all _____ without any help.

3 The detective became famous after catching a serial _____.

4 We found _____ to prove that he committed the bank robbery.

5 They think that the _____ of their new device need to be improved.

6 Something strange happened again and again, and I couldn't _____ what was going on.

C Find the word that has a similar meaning to the underlined word.

1 The research will be underlined carried out over a period of 13 years.

    a. completed   *b.* funded   *c.* kept   *d.* conducted

2 It is important to eat well and exercise to avoid becoming overweight.

    a. thin   *b.* small   *c.* obese   *d.* strong

Dreams

The brain is an amazing organ. Each night, it is able to create vivid images of places and situations that seem real. This is the world of dreams. For centuries, people had many theories about dreams. With the development of brain-scanning technology over the past few decades, we are now able to
5 understand several facts about our dreams.

During sleep, some parts of the brain become very active. With so much activity going on in the brain, it seems that remembering dreams would be easy. But in reality, people remember less than five percent of their dreams. ① This is because some parts of the brain are reactivated during
10 sleep while others are not, changing the brain's chemistry. ② Due to these chemical changes, the content of dreams is stored in short-term memory and cannot be transferred over to long-term memory. ③ There are a few ways to improve your long-term memory. ④ Consequently, it is not possible to remember your dreams unless you record them shortly after waking up.

15 Another characteristic of dreams is how _____ (A) _____

they can be. While we dream, the part of the brain responsible for logical thinking shuts off, and the emotional part of the brain takes over. This is why our dreams are often filled with highly emotional but unusual content. For instance, you may dream about flying like Superman high up in the sky or having an exciting adventure with your favorite cartoon characters. In the world of dreams, anything we can imagine becomes possible.

Recent advances in technology have allowed scientists to better understand how dreams are created. Nevertheless, more studies are needed to fully know the relationship between dreams and the brain.

1 What is the passage mainly about?

    a. How to interpret our dreams

    b. What dreams are made up of

    c. How our brain functions when we dream

    d. How to remember dreams for a long time

2 The difficulty in remembering dreams is caused by _____ during sleep.

    a. additional brain activity

    b. the odd content of dreams

    c. chemical changes in the brain

    d. the emotional part of the brain

3 Which sentence is NOT needed in the passage?

    a. ①   *b.* ②   *c.* ③   *d.* ④

4 What is the best choice for blank (A)?

    a. real or vivid

    b. dark or colorful

    c. random and illogical

    d. normal and expected

5 Why do our dreams have highly emotional but unusual content?

_____

6 Write T if the statement is true or F if it's false.

    1) People usually remember only half of their dreams.

    2) Thanks to modern technology, scientists have discovered all the secrets of dreams.

Fill in the blanks with the correct words.

In the past, people wondered about the cause of dreams. Today we have a better understanding about dreams and the brain. First, the brain becomes very _____ during sleep. Some parts of the brain are reactivated while others remain shut off. This situation causes _____ changes in the brain that prevent dreams from being stored in _____ memory. Dreams are also often filled with unusual and _____ content, such as flying like Superman. This is due to the fact that the _____ portion of the brain shuts off during sleep.

| long-term | active | logical | short-term | chemical | illogical |

★ EXPANDING KNOWLEDGE ★

Do animals dream? Sleeping animals act like they are dreaming by twitching their eyelids and moving their legs and paws. If they do dream, what kinds of dreams do they have and for what purpose?

Scientists studied rats to determine what they dream about. In the study, researchers monitored the brain activity of rats running through a maze. They found that the rats had unique brain activity patterns in each portion of the maze. The researchers then examined the animals' brain activity while they were sleeping. They discovered that about half the rats showed the same brain patterns as when running the maze. This suggests that the rats were practicing running through the maze in their dreams, and doing so enabled them to be more prepared to complete the actual maze.

This study suggests not only that most animals are capable of dreaming, but that they also have more complex dreams than previously thought.

1 How did the research proceed?

a. By monitoring rat races in a maze
b. By analyzing rats' sleeping patterns
c. By examining the brain activity of rats
d. By watching rats' reactions in certain conditions

2 The study suggests that animals _____.

a. dream more often than we thought
b. dream about real-world experiences
c. like to practice running through mazes
d. move their bodies when they are dreaming

70

VOCABULARY REVIEW

A Write the correct word next to its definition.

reactivate	take over	portion	random	transfer

1 a part of something larger: _____

2 to make something start working again: _____

3 happening or chosen without any plan or pattern: _____

4 to move someone or something from one place to another: _____

B Complete each sentence with a word in the box. (Change the form if needed.)

complete	twitch	content	capable of	eyelid	long-term	in reality

1 It looks easy, but _____, it is very difficult.

2 His plan is to _____ all the courses in three years.

3 When I called its name, the cat _____ its ears slightly.

4 This train is _____ carrying more than 500 passengers.

5 My _____ grew heavy, and I couldn't help falling asleep.

6 The _____ effects of stress can be dangerous to your health.

C Find the word that has a similar meaning to the underlined word.

1 I still have vivid memories of my childhood.

    a. vague   *b.* painful   *c.* clear   *d.* wonderful

2 This book describes the technical advances that have taken place since 1990.

    a. changes   *b.* experts   *c.* problems   *d.* developments

Before Reading

Do you think mental power is important in recovering from an illness?

Placebo Effect

When we feel ill, taking medicine usually makes us feel better. But in some cases, just thinking that we are taking medicine is enough to make the pain go away.

5 Known as a placebo, this kind of fake treatment has been used by doctors and researchers for a long time. Amazingly, the "placebo effect" often leaves patients feeling better and experiencing improved health.

10 Placebos can come in many forms, including sugar pills, fake creams, and other substances. They are often used in experiments by researchers testing drugs. The researchers give some patients a placebo and others a real drug. This lets them determine how well a drug works. But how can taking a sugar pill make someone feel better?

15 When you take medicine, your brain expects something positive to happen. The expectation of receiving a reward, such as a relief from pain, causes your brain to release dopamine, a special chemical that makes you feel good. The same brain process occurs when you take fake medicine like a placebo. Just thinking that your pain is going to go away prompts the

20 brain to release these natural painkillers and actually helps get rid of it.

Of course, placebos cannot act as a replacement for real medical treatment. However, by understanding how the placebo effect works, scientists might be able to find new ways to help patients who are

experiencing pain. Perhaps in the future, instead of prescribing potentially dangerous drugs to make patients feel better, doctors will have a way of encouraging patients' brains to get rid of pain naturally.

1 **What is the passage mainly about?**

    a. How placebos work
    b. How placebos are made
    c. Where placebos are used
    d. Whom placebos have an effect on

2 **Why do medical researchers use placebos in their experiments?**

    a. To control pain
    b. To analyze the brain
    c. To see if a drug is effective
    d. To replace an expensive drug

3 **Placebos are effective because our anticipation of _____ triggers the release of natural painkillers.**

    a. destroying a virus
    b. taking more medicine
    c. having our pain reduced
    d. getting special treatments

4 **What is NOT true about dopamine?**

    a. It is a chemical substance released by the brain.
    b. It makes us feel less pain.
    c. It is released by taking placebos.
    d. It is the main ingredient of painkillers.

5 **In the future, thanks to placebos, it might be possible for doctors to treat pain by _____ .**

6 **Write T if the statement is true or F if it's false.**

    1) Placebos can take various forms.
    2) Research shows that placebos are more effective than real medicine.

Fill in the blanks with the correct words.

We usually take medicine to _____ pain. But sometimes just believing that we are taking medicine is _____ to make us feel better. This is called the placebo effect. How do placebos work? When we take medicine, our brain releases dopamine, a special chemical that reduces pain. The _____ thing happens when we take a placebo. The brain anticipates relief and releases its _____ painkiller. While placebos cannot _____ medical treatment, they may help doctors someday understand how our own brains can treat pain.

> enough   relieve   replace   natural   same   prompt

★ EXPANDING KNOWLEDGE ★

Recently, a team of scientists fed a group of rats a lot of junk food to determine what role the brain plays in obesity.

Scientist Paul Johnson and his team found that the more junk food the rats ate, the more the animals wanted to eat in general. This behavior is very similar to drug addiction and suggests that the brain chemistry of obesity and drug addiction may be similar. To prove this, the scientists studied the pleasure center of the rats' brains. They found that the rats that ate junk food needed to eat much more in order to feel pleasure than the rats that consumed a normal diet. This loss of _____(A)_____ is a clear sign of addiction. Ultimately, the rats that were fed junk food refused to give up their unhealthy diet.

This study has helped scientists understand how chemicals in the brain cause people to overeat and gain weight.

1 What is the best choice for blank (A)?

a. control   *b.* balance   *c.* pleasure   *d.* appetite

2 Eating junk food causes obesity because it makes the brain _____.

    a. less interested in losing weight

    b. less sensitive to feeling satisfied

    c. more active in promoting digestion

    d. more stressed about eating healthy food

VOCABULARY REVIEW

A Write the correct word next to its definition.

relief	painkiller	loss	chemistry	replacement

1 the state of not having something anymore: _____

2 the reduction of pain, discomfort, or anxiety: _____

3 a medicine that reduces or removes physical pain: _____

4 someone or something that takes the place of another: _____

B Complete each sentence with a word in the box. (Change the form if needed.)

reward	addiction	feed	overeat	expectation	get rid of	prompt

1 You'll have a stomachache if you _____.

2 The _____ of privacy in public places is unreasonable.

3 The best _____ for a hard day's work is a good night's sleep.

4 He plays games all day long, and his _____ to them looks serious.

5 She said her experience in Nepal _____ her to write her first novel.

6 A large quantity of crude oil was released into the sea. We need to _____ it.

C Find the word that has a similar meaning to the underlined word.

1 I can't get medical treatment because I don't have enough money.

a. advice   b. method   c. drug   d. care

2 You can see fake designer bags in street markets.

a. used   b. false   c. latest   d. unique

Carbohydrate Addiction

Dear Dr. Jay,

I try my best to eat a healthy diet. But sometimes late at night, or even right after a meal, I experience a strong hunger for bread or pasta. Why do I get these cravings, and what can I do to avoid them?

Bella

Dear Bella,

I think I know what the problem is. You have a carbohydrate addiction. You can find carbohydrates in everything from cake to spaghetti to broccoli. (①)

10　When you eat these foods, your body uses insulin to break down the carbohydrates into simpler forms of sugar, which provide energy. (②) There's nothing wrong with that. (③) But eating a lot of carbohydrates raises the body's level of insulin, causing you to consume the carbohydrate sugar too quickly. (④) You're

15　now stuck in an addictive cycle of eating more and more carbohydrates. Like any addiction, this habit is unhealthy. All that carbohydrate sugar can lead to serious diseases like obesity, diabetes, and heart disease.

However, it is still important to eat food with carbohydrates. In recent years, so-called "zero-carb" diets have been very popular. But, the

20　truth is that these diets can be as unhealthy as a carbohydrate addiction. Carbohydrates aren't evil. Experts say carbohydrates should make up about half of the calories in your diet. Most fruits and vegetables containing carbohydrates are also rich in vitamins, minerals, fibers, and other healthy substances. So cutting fruits and vegetables out of your diet just because

25　they have carbohydrates means you're also cutting out lots of healthy stuff. The best thing to do is eat carbohydrates in moderation and be sure that some of them come from foods like fruits, vegetables, grains, and low-fat dairy, which have additional healthy elements.

Dr. Jay

1 What is Bella's problem?

   a. Diet addiction
   b. Failure to lose weight
   c. Eating too much late at night
   d. Strong desire for certain foods

2 Where would the following sentence best fit?

   > This results in hunger because your body thinks it needs to replace all the sugar you're using.

   a. ①   b. ②   c. ③   d. ④

3 What is NOT true about carbohydrates?

   a. They are made up of units of sugar.
   b. They can be used as a source of energy.
   c. Eating too much of them reduces a person's insulin level.
   d. They are often blamed for obesity and other diseases.

4 What can be inferred about a zero-carb diet?

   a. It excludes carbohydrate foods.
   b. It causes a carbohydrate addiction.
   c. It is recommended for diabetic patients.
   d. It involves eating only vegetables and fruits.

5 Why shouldn't fruits and vegetables be completely cut out of your diet?

   _____

6 Write T if the statement is true or F if it's false.

   1) Vegetables and fruits are foods free of carbohydrates.
   2) Grains and low-fat dairy provide carbohydrates in a healthy way.

Fill in the blanks with the correct words.

Carbohydrate Addiction

How it happens
- Eat a lot of carbohydrates → Raises the _____ of insulin in the body → Results in _____ → Want more carbohydrates

Zero-carb diets
- Unhealthy because carbohydrates are a main _____ of energy
- Also cuts out a variety of _____ substances in food

Best solution: Eat carbohydrates, but in _____.

hunger   amount   moderation   source   obesity   healthy

★ EXPANDING KNOWLEDGE ★

People who drink diet cola and still gain weight can blame their poor diets. For instance, someone who eats a healthy diet can lose weight by drinking diet cola in place of regular cola. However, a person who drinks diet cola in order to compensate for eating high-calorie foods will continue to gain weight. These people mistakenly believe that drinking diet cola will allow them to eat whatever they want, so they end up consuming a lot more calories than they would if they were to drink a regular cola. Moreover, new evidence shows that drinking diet cola can stimulate your appetite and increase cravings for sugary foods; thus, it causes indirect weight gain. Overall, if you want to lose weight, drinking water and eating a healthy diet is the best solution.

1 What is the passage mainly about?

a. Diet cola addiction

b. A myth about diet cola

c. Unhealthy eating habits

d. The popularity of diet cola

2 What is NOT true according to the passage?

a. Diet cola can be helpful along with a healthy diet.

b. Drinking diet cola is used as an excuse for consuming more calories.

c. Diet cola causes loss of appetite.

d. It's better to substitute water for diet cola.

VOCABULARY REVIEW

A Write the correct word next to its definition.

| replace | craving | dairy | element | stimulate |

1 foods that are made from milk: _____

2 a very strong desire for something: _____

3 to make something become more active: _____

4 an important or basic part of something: _____

B Complete each sentence with a word in the box. (Change the form if needed.)

| compensate for | appetite | obesity | grain | in place of | break down | in moderation |

1 Food is _____ in the stomach.

2 It is healthy to use sugar and salt _____.

3 Diane served chocolate cake _____ apple pie for dessert.

4 Her excellent language abilities will _____ her lack of experience.

5 Drinking green tea helps curb your _____ and burn more calories.

6 Childhood _____ has become a major health problem in the United States.

C Find the word that has a similar meaning to the underlined word.

1 Overall, this book is very useful.

    a. Partly   *b.* Surely   *c.* Generally   *d.* Fortunately

2 Is it safe to consume American beef?

    a. eat   *b.* buy   *c.* cook   *d.* produce

Derinkuyu Underground City

Before visiting this UNESCO World Heritage Site, I did a little research online. One website described rooms connected like a maze and corridors that restrict movement with darkness and damp air. I wondered how long I could stay in such a place. Its name, Derinkuyu underground city, made me
5 imagine some sort of futuristic town. But it was actually built by Christians as a place to hide from the Roman Empire in the 4th century and Islamic oppression in the 7th century.

Once inside, I followed my guide carefully, as only he knew the way out. I crawled or walked bent over through bedrooms, kitchens, storage
10 rooms, schools, and stables. I had read that only 10 percent of the complex was open to the public, yet it seemed to be endless. My guide explained that this 10 percent is 85 meters deep and has eight floors. The entire complex, he said, can house 20,000 to 50,000 people. I couldn't contain my surprise when I heard that one narrow tunnel leads to another underground city
15 several kilometers away. _____(A)_____ the many oil lamps burning, I could breathe so comfortably that I almost forgot that I was several floors underground.

The most impressive feature was a giant door built to defend the underground city against enemy attacks. It can be opened and closed from
20 the inside but not from the outside. It made me think of the hardship that these people faced. Although this hardship put them in hiding from the sun, their religious conviction allowed them to overcome it and survive.

1 What is the best title for the passage?

    a. How People Can Survive in an Underground City

    b. The Unsolved Mysteries of the Underground City

    c. Impressive Features of UNESCO World Heritage Sites

    d. Heritage Site Protected Deep Faith Deep Underground

2 What can be inferred from the underlined sentence?

    a. Only small people could live in the city.

    b. Visitors should show respect by lowering their bodies.

    c. The Derinkuyu city tour is appropriate for young children.

    d. The ceilings were too low for a person to stand up straight.

3 What is the best choice for blank (A)?

    a. Due to   *b.* Despite

    c. Instead of   *d.* In addition to

4 What feature of the large door in Derinkuyu impressed the writer?

_____

5 What is NOT true about Derinkuyu?

    a. It was built by Christians to escape religious oppression.

    b. Just a small part of it is open to the public.

    c. It is connected to another underground city by several paths.

    d. It had a special device to defend against enemies.

6 Write T if the statement is true or F if it's false.

    1) Derinkuyu underground city is on UNESCO's World Heritage list.

    2) Derinkuyu underground city is huge enough to accommodate lots of people.

Fill in the blanks with the correct words.

STRATEGIC SUMMARY

Derinkuyu underground city was built by Christians to escape _____ persecution during the 4th and 7th centuries. The city, a UNESCO World Heritage Site, is like a(n) _____ of underground corridors and rooms. Visitors can only see 10 percent of the city, which could _____ up to 50,000 people. The city is even _____ to another underground city via a narrow tunnel. But perhaps the most astonishing feature is the _____ defense door that only opens from the inside.

> accommodate   connected   attack   maze   enormous   religious

★ EXPANDING KNOWLEDGE ★

One of the most remote places of worship in the world is the Meteora in Greece. Built on the tops of several peaks, it has been a UNESCO World Heritage Site since 1988.

The Meteora means "middle of the sky" or "suspended in the air" in Greek. Then why and by whom were these structures perched on high cliffs? During the 11th century, monks lived in caves in the area. But after Turkey invaded Greece, the caves became unsafe, so the monks moved higher and higher on the rocks. _____(A)_____ they moved to the peaks where they constructed permanent buildings to conduct their prayers. At the time, the monks used ladders and baskets to bring both materials and people to the top of the peaks. It was not until the 19th and 20th centuries that roads leading to the top were built.

1 What is the best choice for blank (A)?

  a. However   b. Eventually
  c. Furthermore   d. Nevertheless

2 What is NOT mentioned about the Meteora?

  a. Where it is located
  b. Why it was built
  c. Who built it
  d. When it was discovered

VOCABULARY REVIEW

A Write the correct word next to its definition.

restrict	heritage	conviction	conduct	empire

1 a strong belief or opinion: _____

2 to limit or control the movement of someone or something: _____

3 a group of countries that are controlled by one ruler or government: _____

4 the historically important traditions, buildings, and values of a society: _____

B Complete each sentence with a word in the box. (Change the form if needed.)

defend	impressive	endless	remote	oppression	comfortably	permanent

1 The last scene of the movie was really _____.

2 As a result of the accident, he suffered _____ brain damage.

3 Our duty as soldiers is to _____ our country against all threats.

4 Many people around the world fight against government _____.

5 He was tired of answering _____ questions about himself for hours.

6 The earthquake was in a(n) _____ place, so there were no casualties.

C Find the word that has a similar meaning to the underlined word.

1 A huge lamp was <u>suspended</u> from the ceiling.

　　a. lit　　　　　*b.* hung　　　　　*c.* fallen　　　　　*d.* stopped

2 I find it difficult to <u>contain</u> my anger when we have a big argument.

　　a. control　　　*b.* express　　　　*c.* release　　　　*d.* feel

Biodiversity

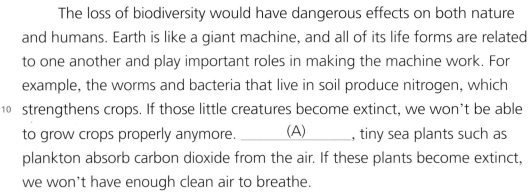

As more and more plants and animals become extinct, biodiversity — the variety of life forms on Earth — declines. Unless we do more to protect the natural habitats of plants and animals, about 30% of all natural
5 life forms will be extinct by 2050. What effect will this have?

The loss of biodiversity would have dangerous effects on both nature and humans. Earth is like a giant machine, and all of its life forms are related to one another and play important roles in making the machine work. For example, the worms and bacteria that live in soil produce nitrogen, which
10 strengthens crops. If those little creatures become extinct, we won't be able to grow crops properly anymore. _____(A)_____, tiny sea plants such as plankton absorb carbon dioxide from the air. If these plants become extinct, we won't have enough clean air to breathe.

Biodiversity also plays a vital role in maintaining human health. A wide
15 variety of life forms are used to produce medicine. Around a quarter of the medicines that we currently use, including antibiotics, contain natural organisms. Also, many other medicines, such as painkillers and penicillin, were created through analysis of natural organisms. Thus, _____(B)_____ organisms we have on Earth, _____(C)_____ it will be to develop new
20 medicines in the future.

In short, if biodiversity were lost, the world would be a very different place. Things like nitrogen for soil and medicine for sick people would become extremely expensive as supplies ran low, and countries would have to compete with each other for access to them. This could lead to many
25 problems, and even wars. Thus, we should do something to protect Earth's biodiversity, or life will get worse.

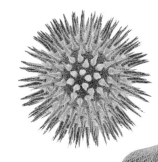

1 What is the best title for the passage?

    a. The Use of Biodiversity

    b. What If We Lose Biodiversity?

    c. Ways of Conserving Biodiversity

    d. Climate Change and Biodiversity

2 What is the best choice for blank (A)?

    a. Similarly   *b.* In contrast

    c. As a result   *d.* Nevertheless

3 Why is biodiversity important in the development of medical science?

_____

4 What is the best pair for blanks (B) and (C)?

	(B)		(C)
a.	the fewer	—	the easier
b.	the fewer	—	the more difficult
c.	the more	—	the worse
d.	the more	—	the more necessary

5 What is NOT mentioned as a possible result of the loss of biodiversity?

    a. The growth of crop plants will become worse.

    b. The quality of the air will be poor.

    c. Producing medicines will cost a lot of money.

    d. There will be an overpopulation of microorganisms.

6 Write T if the statement is true or F if it's false.

    1) Almost all new medicines are produced from natural organisms.

    2) Biodiversity loss can eventually cause conflict between countries.

STRATEGIC SUMMARY

Fill in the blanks with the correct words.

Biodiversity is important because human life depends on _____.
For example, the nitrogen produced by worms in the dirt helps crops to
grow. If worms became _____, people couldn't grow healthy
crops. Moreover, biodiversity contributes to making medicine. Many of
our medicines either contain natural organisms or are made from the
_____ of natural organisms. A(n) _____ of biodiversity
could eventually result in competition for food and medicine, and perhaps,
in the future, there will be wars between countries to _____ for
resources.

> lack   compete   nature   strengthen   extinct   analysis

★ EXPANDING KNOWLEDGE ★

Although we think of the Arctic and Antarctic as
empty, lifeless places where only polar bears and
penguins can survive, over 200 different species now
live there. In fact, the level of biodiversity is higher in
the Antarctic than in the Galapagos Islands, which
are famous for the range of species living there. In
the Arctic and Antarctic, scientists found whales,
birds, worms, and many other animals. They believe that animals are moving to these
areas because global warming has made them seek cooler habitats. In addition, some
parts of the sea are now exposed to sunlight for the first time in 100,000 years due to
the melting of the ice. Scientists from around the world are using high-tech methods
to study sea creatures and discover more about the oceans. There is a large amount of
information to learn about life in the poles.

1 What is the best title for the passage?

   a. Lifeless Areas on Earth   *b.* Melting the Ends of Earth

   c. Biodiversity at the Ends of Earth   *d.* Biodiversity and Global Warming

2 Write T if the statement is true or F if it's false.

   1) Global warming plays a role in biodiversity changes at the poles.

   2) Antarctica is richer in biodiversity than the Galapagos Islands.

Unit ⋆ 20
VOCABULARY REVIEW

A Write the correct word next to its definition.

antibiotic	variety	breathe	analysis	habitat

1 to inhale and exhale air through the nose or mouth: _____

2 the natural environment where a plant or animal lives: _____

3 a medicine that destroys or inhibits the growth of bacteria: _____

4 a process of examining something in detail in order to understand it: _____

B Complete each sentence with a word in the box. (Change the form if needed.)

absorb	compete	species	extinct	range	melt	lifeless

1 The university offers a wide _____ of classes to choose from.

2 The scientists discovered another cold, _____ planet in the universe.

3 This theory explains why dinosaurs became _____ millions of years ago.

4 The best soccer teams will _____ with each other to win the World Cup.

5 I wonder how many _____ of plants are able to grow in desert conditions.

6 The teacher explained how flowers _____ water and nutrients from the soil.

C Find the word that has a similar meaning to the underlined word.

1 It is extremely difficult to predict earthquakes.

a. very   b. simply   c. sometimes   d. hardly

2 Entering the American market successfully is vital to the company's survival.

a. helpful   b. related   c. essential   d. urgent

MEMO

NE능률의 모든 교재가 한 곳에 - 엔이 북스

NE_Books

www.nebooks.co.kr ▼

NE능률의 유초등 교재부터 중고생 참고서,
토익·토플 수험서와 일반 영어까지!
PC는 물론 태블릿 PC, 스마트폰으로 언제 어디서나
NE능률의 교재와 다양한 학습 자료를 만나보세요.

✓ 필요한 부가 학습 자료 바로 찾기
✓ 주요 인기 교재들을 한눈에 확인
✓ 나에게 딱 맞는 교재를 찾아주는 스마트 검색
✓ 함께 보면 좋은 교재와 다음 단계 교재 추천
✓ 회원 가입, 교재 후기 작성 등 사이트 활동 시 NE Point 적립

건강한
배움의 즐거움

영어교과서 리딩튜터 능률보카 빠른독해 바른독해 수능만만 월등한 개념 수학 유형더블 토마토 토익 NE 클래스
NE_Build & Grow   NE_Times   NE_Kids(굿잡,상상수프)   NE_능률 주니어랩   아이챌린지

NE 능률

Reading FORWARD

ADVANCED 2

★ Answer Key ★

Reading FORWARD

ADVANCED 2

★ Answer Key ★

The U.S. Dollar Coin

1 b **2** c **3** a, b **4** Because she knew several Indian languages and was familiar with many native tribes. **5** b **6** b

당신에게 아무 동전이나 지폐가 있다면, 하나의 앞면을 자세히 보라. 누가 등장하는가? 일반적으로, 화폐에 등장하도록 선택되는 인물은 한 나라의 사람들에게 중요하다고 여겨지고, 그들은 보통 영국의 엘리자베스 2세 여왕이나 한국의 세종대왕처럼 유명한 지도자들이었다. 그러나 미국은 1달러 동전에 뭔가 다른 일을 했다.

Sacagawea 달러 동전은 1달러의 가치가 있고, 15세 북미 원주민 소녀의 모습을 담고 있다. 그것은 특별 대통령 주화와 함께 2000년부터 발행되고 있다. 그런데 이 동전에는 특별한 점이 하나 더 있다. 2007년에 북미 원주민의 역사를 더욱 기리기 위해 북미 원주민 1달러 주화법이 통과되었다. 그 법은 특별한 Sacagawea 동전이 2010년대 내내 발행될 것을 요구했다. 이 기간 동안 매년, 그 동전의 뒷면에는 다양한 북미 원주민 부족과 관련된 주제를 묘사하는 서로 다른 이미지가 담길 것이다.

그런데 Sacagawea가 미국인들에게 그렇게 중요한 이유는 무엇일까? 십 대의 나이에도 불구하고 그녀는 여러 가지 인디언 언어를 알았고 많은 원주민 부족과도 친숙했다. 이런 이유로 그녀는 역사적인 Lewis와 Clark 탐험대에 고용되었고, 그들은 1804년부터 1806년까지 미 서부를 탐험했다. Sacagawea는 북부 대평원에서부터 태평양까지의 왕복 여행을 따라 Lewis와 Clark를 성공적으로 안내했다. 그녀의 도움이 없었더라면, 탐험가들은 틀림없이 죽었을 것이다.

이상하게도, Sacagawea가 실제로 어떻게 생겼는지 아는 사람은 아무도 없다. 그녀는 25세의 나이에 죽었고, 그녀에 대한 어떤 사진이나 묘사도 발견된 적이 없다. 동전에 있는 이미지는 대략 같은 나이와 배경을 가진 북미 원주민 모델을 토대로 한 것이었다. 비록 그 이미지가 완전히 정확하지는 않지만, 그것은 여전히 미국 역사의 훌륭한 일면을 보여준다!

어휘 figure[fígjər] 몡 숫자; *인물   currency[kə́:rənsi] 몡 화폐   feature[fí:tʃər] 통 특별히 포함하다, 특징으로 삼다   issue[íʃu:] 통 발행하다   presidential[prèzədénʃəl] 혱 대통령의   act[ækt] 몡 행동; *법률   pass[pæs] 통 지나가다; *(법률을) 통과시키다   depict[dipíkt] 통 묘사하다   theme[θi:m] 몡 주제   tribe[traib] 몡 부족   historic[histɔ́:rik] 혱 역사적으로 중요한   expedition[èkspədíʃən] 몡 탐험   explore[iksplɔ́:r] 통 탐험하다 (explorer 몡 탐험가)   description[diskrípʃən] 몡 묘사   be based on …에 바탕을 두다   roughly[rʌ́fli] 튀 대략   accurate[ǽkjurət] 혱 정확한   represent[rèprizént] 통 대표하다; *나타내다   [문제] call for (공식적으로) 요구하다

구문 3행 Generally, **the figures** [*selected* to appear on currency] **are considered important** by the people of a country, ….
• consider + 목적어 + 형용사: '…을 ~라고 여기다'의 의미로, 목적어(the figures)가 주어로 변환된 수동태 문장
• selected 이하는 the figures를 수식하는 과거분사구

12행 But there is one more thing [**that** *makes* it *special*].
• that 이하는 one more thing을 수식하는 주격 관계대명사절
• make + 목적어 + 형용사: …을 ~하게 하다

15행 …, the back of the coin will feature a different image, (which is) **depicting** themes ….
• depicting 앞에 '주격 관계대명사 + be동사'가 생략되어 있음

19행 … the historic Lewis and Clark Expedition, **which** explored the Western U.S. from 1804 to 1806.

- which: Lewis and Clark Expedition을 보충 설명하는 계속적 용법의 주격 관계대명사

23행 **Without** her help, the explorers surely **would have died**.
  - '…가 없었다면, ~했을 텐데'의 의미의 가정법 과거완료 문장으로, without이 이끄는 구가 if절을 대신함(= If it had not been for her help)

24행 Strangely, no one knows [**what** Sacagawea really looked like].
  - what 이하는 '의문사 + 주어 + 동사' 어순의 간접의문문으로, 동사 knows의 목적어 역할을 함

STRATEGIC SUMMARY   leaders, guided, different, record, background

EXPANDING KNOWLEDGE

1 a   **2** c

미국 화폐의 가장 흔한 형태는 1달러 지폐인데, 그것은 1862년에 처음 만들어졌다. 달러 지폐는 1달러의 가치가 있으며, 1869년 이래로 미국의 초대 대통령인 조지 워싱턴의 모습이 실렸다. 달러 지폐가 발행되기 전에, 달러 화폐는 1794년에 처음 등장한 동전이었다. 오늘날에는, 여러 다양한 달러 주화가 유통되고 있다. 그중 가장 오래된 것이 Susan B. Anthony 동전이다. 그것은 1979년부터 유통되고 있으며 그것의 이름을 딴 유명한 여성 사회 운동가의 모습을 담고 있다. 그것은 여전히 사용할 수 있으나 더 이상 생산되지는 않는다. 사람들이 종종 그 동전을 비슷하게 생긴 25센트짜리와 혼동해서, 정부는 이후의 달러 주화를 모두 금색으로 만들었다. 이러한 동전에는 역대 미국 대통령을 기리는 대통령 달러 주화와 Sacagawea 동전으로도 알려진 북미 원주민 주화가 포함된다. 이들 달러 주화는 현재 달러 지폐와 함께 모두 사용되고 있다.

어휘   prior to …의 전에   release[rilíːs] 몡 출시, 발행   in circulation (화폐 따위가) 유통되고 있는, 현재 쓰이고 있는   social activist 사회 운동가   available[əvéiləbl] 혱 구할 수 있는, 사용 가능한   confuse[kənfjúːz] 동 혼동하다   quarter[kwɔ́ːrtər] 몡 4분의 1; *25센트짜리 동전   former[fɔ́ːrmər] 혱 이전의   currently[kə́ːrəntli] 분 현재, 지금

구문   9행   … the image of the famous female social activist [**for whom** it is named].
  - for whom 이하는 the famous female social activist를 수식하는 목적격 관계대명사절

11행   These include the presidential dollar coins [**honoring** former U.S. presidents] and the Native American coin [**also known as** the Sacagawea coin].
  - honoring 이하는 the presidential dollar coins를 수식하는 현재분사구
  - also known as 이하는 the Native American coin을 수식하는 과거분사구

VOCABULARY REVIEW

A   **1** feature   **2** currency   **3** figure   **4** description
B   **1** historic   **2** prior to   **3** presidential   **4** expedition   **5** honor   **6** issued
C   **1** a   **2** c

unit
02 ENTERTAINMENT pp. 12-15

★Movie Posters

1 c   **2** They try to create an image that both intrigues viewers and gives them some facts about the movie.   **3** d   **4** c   **5** d   **6** *1)* T   *2)* T

영화를 홍보하기 위해 포스터를 이용하는 것은 오랜 전통이지만, 21세기에는 포스터가 영향을 미치려면 정말로 눈에 띄어야 한다. 그렇지 않으면, 그것은 단지 우리의 일상 속 상업적인 배경의 또 다른 일부로 간과될 것이다. 포스터를 디자인할 때, 디자이너는 보는 사람들의 흥미를 불러일으키고 그들에게 영화에 대한 몇 가지 사실을 제공하는 이미지를 만들어내려고 애쓴다.

영화 포스터는 보통 세 가지 스타일 중 하나에 속한다. 첫 번째는 티저 포스터이다. 티저 포스터는 정보를 많이 제공하지 않는데, 그 대신 우리가 더 많이 알고 싶어지게 하는 영화의 흥미로운 장면이나 핵심 문구를 넣는 것이 특징이다. 또 다른 흔한 스타일은 캐릭터 포스터인데, 그것은 영화 주인공의 모습에 초점을 맞춘다. 영화 300의 포스터가 이러한 스타일을 보여준다. 그것은 전투 의상을 입고 적에게 소리를 지르는 주인공을 보여준다. 마지막으로, 예술적 포스터가 있다. 이는 좀 더 추상적이며, 예술적인 이미지를 통해 영화의 주제나 감정을 보여주려 한다.

유형에 관계없이, 포스터는 보통 영화의 장르에 대한 단서를 제공한다. 예를 들어, 슈퍼히어로 영화의 포스터는 로맨틱 코미디의 포스터와는 매우 다르게 보인다. 만약 밤에 으스스한 언덕 위의 어둡고 인적이 없는 집 한 채가 있는 포스터를 보게 되고, 그것의 글이 꾸불꾸불하고 유령 같은 서체로 쓰여 있다면, 당신은 그것이 공포 영화를 광고한다는 것을 알게 된다.

영화 포스터가 단지 홍보 그 이상이라는 것은 명백하다. 영화 포스터의 주된 목적은 우리의 관심을 사로잡고 우리로 하여금 그 영화를 보게 하는 것이다. 하지만 영화 포스터는 또한 영화의 비밀은 알려주지 않으면서 영화의 내용에 대해 암시해 줄 필요가 있다. 그것은 단 하나의 이미지로 하기는 힘든 일이다!

어휘　promote[prəmóut] ⑧ 홍보하다 (promotion ⑱ 홍보)　stand out 두드러지다
overlook[òuvərlúk] ⑧ 간과하다　commercial[kəmə́ːrʃəl] ⑱ 상업적인　intrigue[intríːg]
⑧ 흥미를 불러 일으키다　tag line 핵심 구절　demonstrate[démənstrèit] ⑧ 증명하다;
*보여주다　abstract[æbstrǽkt] ⑱ 추상적인　illustrate[íləstrèit] ⑧ 삽화를 넣다; *분명히 보여주다
regardless of …에 상관없이　clue[kluː] ⑱ 단서　lonesome[lóunsəm] ⑱ 외로운; *인적이 드문
spooky[spúːki] ⑱ 으스스한, 귀신이 나올 것 같은　wavy[wéivi] ⑱ 물결 모양의　capture[kǽptʃər]
⑧ 포로로 잡다; *(관심을) 사로잡다　content[kántent] ⑱ 내용　give away 거저 주다; *(비밀 등을)
누설하다　[문제] current[kə́ːrənt] ⑱ 현재의, 지금의　qualification[kwὰləfikéiʃən] ⑱ 자격, 요건
requirement[rikwáiərmənt] ⑱ 필요조건, 요건

구문　5행　[**When designing** a poster], designers try to create an image [that **both**
　　　　　　intrigues viewers **and** gives them some facts about the movie].
　　　　　　• When designing 이하는 때를 나타내는 분사구문으로, 의미를 명확하게 하기 위해 접속사를
　　　　　　　생략하지 않음
　　　　　　• that 이하는 an image를 수식하는 주격 관계대명사절
　　　　　　• both A and B: A와 B 둘 다
　　　　13행　… the character poster, **which** focuses on an image of the film's main character.
　　　　　　• which: the character poster를 보충 설명하는 계속적 용법의 주격 관계대명사
　　　　15행　It shows the main character [**dressed** for battle] and [**yelling** at his enemies].
　　　　　　• dressed와 yelling 이하는 각각 the main character를 수식하는 과거분사구와 현재분사구
　　　　25행　**It**'s clear [**that** movie posters are more than just promotions].
　　　　　　• It은 가주어이고, that 이하가 진주어

STRATEGIC ORGANIZER　interest, abstract, genre, attention, Hint

EXPANDING KNOWLEDGE

1 c　**2** d

영화 초기에는, 영화 포스터가 광고물에 불과하다고 여겨졌다. 영화마다 한정된 수량의 포스터가 제작되었고, 제작 스튜디오는 영화 상영이 끝난 후 극장에 포스터를 반납할 것을 요구하곤 했다.

하지만 2차 세계대전 후, 진지한 영화 팬들은 자신들이 좋아하는 영화의 포스터를 수집하는 것에 큰 관심을 보이기 시작했다. 포스터의 잠재적인 가치를 인식해서, 몇몇 극장 소유주들은 스튜디오의 반납 정책을 무시하기 시작하며, 쓰레기매립지에서 소수의 걸작 포스터들을 살려냈다. 이후, '전지 크기'의 고전 포스터는 수집가가 소장할 수 있는 가장 유명한 영화 기념품으로 변모했다. 1980년대 이래로, 이러한 수집품들이 국제적인 위신을 얻게 되면서 가장 비싼 수집품들은 수백만 달러의 가치를 지니게 되었다.

어휘   nothing more than …에 불과한   run[rʌn] 명 달리기; *장기 상영   collect[kəlékt] 동 수집하다 (collector 명 수집가 collection 명 수집품)   potential[pəténʃəl] 형 잠재적인   vintage[víntidʒ] 형 고급의; *걸작의   landfill[lǽndfìl] 명 쓰레기 매립지   subsequently[sʌ́bsikwəntli] 부 그 후에, 나중에   transform[trænsfɔ́ːrm] 동 변형시키다   renowned[rináund] 형 유명한   souvenir[sùːvəníər] 명 기념품, 선물   prestige[prestíːʒ] 명 위신, 명망   [문제] evaluate[ivǽljuèit] 동 평가하다, 감정하다   distributor[distríbjutər] 명 배급자

구문   3행   … the production studio would **require** that the theater (should) **return** the posters after the film's run *had ended*.
- 요구를 나타내는 동사 require 뒤에 이어지는 that절의 동사는 'should + 동사원형'을 쓰는데, should는 종종 생략됨
- had ended: 주절의 시제보다 앞선 시점의 내용을 가리키는 과거완료

   10행   …, such collections have gained international prestige, **with** the most expensive collections (being) **worth** millions of dollars.
- with + 명사 + v-ing: '…가 ~한 채로'라는 의미의 분사구문으로, worth 앞에 현재분사 being이 생략되어 있음

VOCABULARY REVIEW

A   **1** overlook   **2** intrigue   **3** potential   **4** souvenir
B   **1** transformed   **2** abstract   **3** regardless of   **4** promote   **5** yelled at   **6** illustrate
C   **1** d   **2** b

unit 03 ART

pp. 16-19

Eyes in Paintings

1 c   **2** c   **3** It creates a sense of depth.   **4** b   **5** c   **6** 1) T   2) F

당신은 레오나르도 다빈치의 *모나리자*라는 유명한 그림을 보기 위해 파리에 있는 루브르 박물관에 있다. 그림 속의 여인을 보면서, 당신은 자세히 보려고 좌우로 걷는다. 그런데 갑자기, 다소 무서운 무언가를 알아차린다. 당신이 움직이는 곳마다, *모나리자*의 눈이 당신을 따라다니는 것이다! 그림이 살아 움직이게 된 것일까?

물론, *모나리자*가 살아 있는 것은 아니지만, 그녀는 진짜처럼 보이도록 신중을 기하여 그려졌다. 다빈치는 이를 위해 원근법이라는 기법을 사용했다. 그는 이미지의 특정 부분을 다른 곳보다 더 크게 그려서, 그 부분들이 '더 가깝게' 보이게 했다. 빛과 음영의 사용도 비슷한 효과를 내는데, 빛을 받은 부분은 더 가까이 있는 것 같고, 음영이 드리운 부분은 더 멀리 있는 것처럼 느껴진다. 이러한 기법들은 화가들로 하여금 입체감을 만들어내게 해준다.

하지만 이런 입체감은 일종의 착각이다. 우리가 주변 세계에서 보는 3차원과 비교할 때, 캔버스는 2차원에 지나지 않는다. 그렇지만 당신이 친구의 얼굴을 보며 좌우로 움직일 때, 친구의 시선이 당신을 따라오는가? 물론 아니다.

이는 당신의 시점이 변하고 있기 때문이다. 당신이 이리저리 움직이면, 당신은 서로 다른 거리에서 친구의 눈을 보게 되고, 친구 얼굴의 빛과 그림자는 달라지게 된다. 하지만 그림에서는 원근, 빛, 음영의 특성들이 모든 각도에서 똑같다. 그것들은 변하지 않으며 평면적이다. 이 때문에, 그림의 얼굴이 한쪽 각도에서 당신을 보고 있다면, 그 눈은 다른 모든 각도에서도 당신을 응시할 것이다.

그러므로 초상화의 눈은 무서운 것도 마법에 걸린 것도 아니다. 하지만 유령이 출몰하는 대저택에 있는 그림들은 다르다. 만약 그들의 눈이 당신을 따라오는 것을 본다면, 달아나는 편이 좋다!

어휘 view[vjuː] ⑧ 보다 　detail[ditéil] ⑲ 세부 사항 　scary[skέəri] ⑳ 무서운 　come to life 활기를 띠다; *살아 움직이다 　perspective[pərspéktiv] ⑲ 원근법; 관점, 시각 　section[sékʃən] ⑲ 부분 shadow[ʃǽdou] ⑲ 그림자; *(그림의) 음영 　depth[depθ] ⑲ 깊이; *입체감 　dimension[diménʃən] ⑲ 치수; *차원 　compared to …와 비교하여 　permanent[pə́ːrmənənt] ⑳ 영구적인 　flat[flæt] ⑳ 평면의 　angle[ǽŋgl] ⑲ 각, 각도 　gaze[geiz] ⑧ 응시하다 　portrait[pɔ́ːrtrit] ⑲ 초상화 haunted[hɔ́ːntid] ⑳ 유령이 나오는 　mansion[mǽnʃən] ⑲ 대저택 　[문제] define[difáin] ⑧ 정의를 내리다 　concept[kάnsept] ⑲ 개념 　masterpiece[mǽstərpìːs] ⑳ 걸작, 명작 appreciate[əpríːʃièit] ⑧ 가치를 인정하다; *감상하다 　illusion[ilúːʒən] ⑲ 착각 　relative[rélətiv] ⑳ 상대적인 　perceive[pərsíːv] ⑧ 인지하다

구문 7행 **Wherever** you move, the *Mona Lisa*'s eyes follow you!
　• wherever: '어디로 …하더라도'라는 의미의 복합관계부사(= no matter where)
15행 The use of light and shadow has a similar effect, **with** lit areas **seeming** closer and (with) *those* in shadow **feeling** farther away.
　• with + 명사 + v-ing: '…가 ~한 채로'라는 의미의 분사구문으로, 명사와 분사가 능동 관계일 때 현재분사를 씀
　• those: 앞에 나온 areas를 대신하는 대명사
20행 …, compared to the three (dimensions) [(which[that]) **we see** in the world around us].
　• we see 앞에 the three (dimensions)를 선행사로 하는 목적격 관계대명사가 생략되어 있음
29행 If you **see** their eyes **following** you, you'd *better run*!
　• 지각동사(see) + 목적어 + v-ing: …가 ~하고 있는 것을 보다
　• had better + 동사원형: …하는 편이 낫다, …해야 하다

STRATEGIC SUMMARY perspective, closer, depth, flat, follow

EXPANDING KNOWLEDGE

1 d **2** a

세상에 대해 우리가 이해하는 상당 부분은 우리가 보는 것을 바탕으로 한다. 하지만 때때로 우리가 보는 것은 실제로 존재하는 것이 아니다. 세상에 대한 이러한 부정확한 인지는 착시라고 불린다.

비록 인식하지 못할지도 모르지만, 당신은 거의 매일 착시를 경험한다. 예를 들어, 텔레비전이 만들어내는 수백만 가지의 색상은 빨강, 초록, 파랑, 단 세 가지 색의 결과이다. 화면을 가까이에서 본다면, 당신은 이 세 가지 색을 담고 있는 미세한 점들을 볼 수 있다. 그 색들이 서로 아주 가까이 있기 때문에, 당신의 뇌가 그들을 합쳐서 수없이 많은 다른 색상들을 만들어내는 것이다. 흔히 일어나는 또 다른 착시는 옷의 무늬가 사람을 달라 보이게 하는 방식이다. 예를 들면, 세로줄 무늬나 가로줄 무늬 옷은 사람을 더 날씬하고 키가 더 커 보이게 한다.

따라서 우리의 눈이 우리가 현실을 볼 수 있게 해준다고 믿을지 몰라도, 우리가 보는 것은 종종 사실과 다르다.

어휘 incorrect[ìnkərékt] ⑳ 부정확한 　perception[pərsépʃən] ⑲ 지각 　visual illusion 착시 dot[dat] ⑲ 점 　countless[káuntlis] ⑳ 무수한, 셀 수 없이 많은 　vertical[və́ːrtikəl] ⑳ 수직의, 세로의 horizontal[hɔ̀ːrəzάntl] ⑳ 수평의, 가로의 　stripe[straip] ⑲ 줄무늬 　[문제] objective[əbdʒéktiv]

⑱ 객관적인   process[práses] ⑧ 처리하다   misrepresentation[mìsreprizentéiʃən] ⑲ 그릇된 설명

구문   1행   A large part of our understanding of the world is based on **what** we see.
• what: '···하는 것'의 의미로, 선행사를 포함하는 관계대명사(= the thing which)
10행   Another common visual illusion is **how**[the way] patterns on clothes *make* a person *look* different.
• how: 방법을 나타내는 관계부사로, 선행사 the way와 함께 쓰지 않음
• 사역동사(make) + 목적어 + 동사원형: ···가 ~하게 하다

VOCABULARY REVIEW

A   **1** visual   **2** horizontal   **3** portrait   **4** perception
B   **1** come to life   **2** angles   **3** illusion   **4** combine   **5** vertical   **6** flat
C   **1** d   **2** a

★*unit*
04 **TEENS**   pp. 20-23

★*Stress*

1 b   **2** c   **3** b   **4** when you feel more prepared to face them, you will be less stressed   **5** d
6 *1)* F   *2)* T

힘든 상황을 겪는 중에는 어떤 느낌이 드는가? 아마 심장 박동이 빨라지고, 얼굴이 화끈거리고, 불안감을 겪을 것이다. 이것은 자연스러운 반응이다. 당신이 그 상황을 극복하도록 돕는 방식으로 당신의 몸이 그 상황에 반응하고 있는 것이다. 그러나 때때로 그 상황을 감당할 수 없다고 느끼는데, 그것이 스트레스가 발생하는 때이다.

숙제에서부터 자동차 사고에 이르기까지 우리 삶의 많은 일들이 스트레스를 일으킬 수 있다. 비록 우리는 그 기분을 즐기지 않지만, 스트레스가 항상 부정적인 것만은 아니다. 예를 들어, 당신이 숙제를 끝내는 것에 대해 걱정하고 스트레스가 당신이 숙제를 더 빨리하게 하고 제시간에 끝낼 수 있게 만든다면 문제가 없다. 그러나 당신이 스트레스를 장기간 지속적으로 겪는다면 스트레스는 긍정적이기보다는 부정적이게 된다. 그런 만성적인 스트레스는 심각한 건강 문제이며, 그것에 대처해야만 한다.

스트레스를 낮추는 한 가지 전략은 당신의 하루에 할 일 목록을 간소화하는 것이다. 어떤 과제가 긴급하고 어떤 것이 미뤄져도 되는지 파악하라. 이것은 꼭 필요하지 않은 활동에 대한 스트레스를 줄여줄 것이다. 또 다른 방법은 일기를 쓰는 것이다. 스트레스를 일으키는 상황들에 대해 적고, 그러한 상황들의 모든 가능한 결과를 상상해보라. 그 상황들에 맞설 준비가 더 되어있다고 느끼면, 스트레스가 덜할 것이다. 또한, 스트레스를 풀기 위해 울거나 잠을 더 자기 위해 일정을 조정하는 것의 중요성을 과소평가하지 마라. 이런 신체적인 전략은 당신의 몸이 스트레스 누적에 대처할 수 있도록 도와준다.

스트레스를 줄이는 이런 각각의 방법들을 시험해 보고 자신에게 가장 잘 맞는 방법을 찾거나 자신만의 방법을 만들어보라! 효과가 있는 방법을 발견하게 되면, 종이에 쓰고 그것을 책상 위나 침대 옆에 붙여 두어라. 스트레스를 느낄 때마다, 그 쪽지를 보면 해결책을 갖게 될 것이다!

어휘   heartbeat[háːrtbìːt] ⑲ 심장 박동   anxiety[æŋzáiəti] ⑲ 불안감   reaction[riǽkʃən] ⑲ 반응
respond[rispánd] ⑧ 응답하다; *반응을 보이다   overcome[òuvərkʌ́m] ⑧ 극복하다
overwhelming[òuvərhwélmiŋ] ⑱ 압도적인, 감당할 수 없는   assignment[əsáinmənt]
⑲ 과제, 임무   complete[kəmplíːt] ⑧ 끝내다   continually[kəntínjuəli] ⑼ 지속적으로
chronic[kránik] ⑱ 만성적인   strategy[strǽtədʒi] ⑲ 전략   simplify[símpləfài] ⑧ 간소화하다,

단순화하다   wait[weit] ⑧ 기다리다, *(긴급하지 않으므로) 미뤄지다   keep a journal 일기를 쓰다
underestimate[ʌ̀ndəréstəmeit] ⑧ 과소평가하다   release[rilíːs] ⑧ 놓아주다; *(긴장 등을) 풀다
adjust[ədʒʌ́st] ⑧ 조정하다   aid[eid] ⑧ 돕다   buildup[bíldʌ̀p] ⑨ 축적   relieve[rilíːv] ⑧ 덜어
주다   [문제] restrain[ristréin] ⑧ 억누르다, 참다

구문	8행	..., the situation feels overwhelming, and that is (the time) **when** stress occurs.

· when: 시간을 나타내는 관계부사로, 앞에 선행사 the time이 생략되어 있음

14행　Even though we don't enjoy the feeling, stress is **not always** negative.
　　· not always: '항상 …인 것은 아니다'라는 의미의 부분부정

16행　..., and stress **makes** you **work** faster and **complete** it on time, ...
　　· 사역동사(make) + 목적어 + 동사원형: …가 ~하게 하다

21행　Figure out [**which** tasks are urgent] and [**which** ones can wait].
　　· which: '(제한된 범위에서) 어느[어떤]…'의 의미로, 동사구 figure out의 목적어 역할을 하는
　　　간접의문문을 이끄는 의문형용사
　　· ones: 앞서 언급된 tasks를 대신하는 대명사

25행　... the importance of [**crying** to release stress] or [**adjusting** your schedule to
　　get more sleep].
　　· crying과 adjusting 이하는 각각 전치사 of의 목적어 역할을 하는 동명사구
　　· to release와 to get은 목적을 나타내는 부사적 용법의 to부정사

STRATEGIC ORGANIZER　ability, health, importance, journal, sleep

EXPANDING KNOWLEDGE

1 b　**2** *1)* T *2)* T

우리의 삶에서 극도로 스트레스를 받는 상황에 처할 때가 있다. 이러한 상황들은 우리의 몸과 마음이 스트레스에 대처하는 방식에 장기적인 영향을 미칠 수 있고 우울증과 같은 심각한 정신 장애로 이어질 수 있다.
　스트레스가 너무 심해서 혼자 대처할 수 없다면, 당신은 분명 도움을 구해야 한다. 부모님이나 선생님처럼 당신이 믿을 수 있는 어른들에게 얘기하라. 당신이 겪고 있는 스트레스와 그것이 어떤 영향을 미치고 있는지에 대해 솔직해지라. 이는 혼자라는 느낌을 줄여주고 문제에 대한 해결책을 찾을 수 있게 해준다. 당신은 또한 전문 치료사나 의사, 종교 지도자에게 상담을 받기 원할 수도 있다. 이것이 스트레스의 원인을 최대한 줄이는 데 도움이 될 수 있다.
　당신의 몸이 말하는 것을 이해하는 것은 성장의 중요한 부분이다. 당신이 스트레스로 지칠 때마다 언제든 도움을 구할 수 있다는 것을 기억하라.

어휘　extremely[ikstríːmli] ⑨ 심히, 극도로 (extreme ⑩ 심각한, 극도의)   long-term[lóːŋtə̀ːrm] ⑩ 장기적인
disorder[disɔ́ːrdər] ⑨ 무질서; *장애   depression[dipréʃən] ⑨ 우울증   definitely[défənitli]
⑨ 분명히   counseling[káunsəliŋ] ⑨ 상담   therapist[θérəpist] ⑨ 치료 전문가
religious[rilídʒəs] ⑩ 종교의   minimize[mínəmàiz] ⑧ 최소화하다   stressed out 스트레스로 지친,
심한 스트레스를 받는   available[əvéiləbl] ⑩ 구할 수 있는, 사용 가능한   [문제] address[ədrés]
⑧ 다루다   consult[kənsʌ́lt] ⑧ 상담하다

구문　1행　These situations can have long-term effects on **how**[the way] our bodies and
　　minds deal with stress ....
　　· how: 방법을 나타내는 관계부사로, 선행사 the way와는 함께 쓰지 않음

4행　If your stress is **too** much *for you* **to handle** alone, ...
　　· too ... to-v: 너무 …해서 ~할 수 없다
　　· for you: to부정사의 의미상 주어

5행　Be honest about the stress [(which[that]) **you** are facing] and [*how* it is affecting
　　you].
　　· you 앞에 the stress를 선행사로 하는 목적격 관계대명사가 생략되어 있음

8

VOCABULARY REVIEW

A **1** overwhelming **2** anxiety **3** chronic **4** underestimate
B **1** release **2** simplify **3** continually **4** reaction **5** urgent **6** figure out
C **1** a **2** d

unit *05* SPORTS

pp. 24-27

Soccer Jersey Swap

1 b **2** b **3** a **4** Because opposing players all wanted to swap jerseys with them. **5** d
6 *1)* T *2)* F

축구를 처음으로 보는 사람이라면 마지막 호각 소리가 날 때 일어나는 일에 놀랄지도 모른다. 치열한 시합이 끝난 후, 선수들은 자신의 셔츠를 벗어 상대 팀 선수들과 교환한다. 이것은 이상해 보일 수도 있지만, 이것은 1931년부터 축구의 전통이 되었는데, 이때 프랑스와 영국의 선수들이 경기 종료 후 셔츠를 교환했다.

왜 선수들은 상대 팀 선수들과 셔츠를 교환할까? 이것은 오늘날 경기가 점점 치열해지고 있지만, 페어플레이 정신은 여전히 중요하다는 것을 보여주기 위해서다. 축구에는 당신이 봤을 수도 있는 다른 비슷한 전통들이 있다. 예를 들어, 상대 팀 선수들은 반칙을 한 후 서로 일어나는 것을 도와준다. 또한, 상대 팀 선수가 다치면, 그 선수가 치료를 받을 수 있도록 공을 경기장 밖으로 차 낸다. 마찬가지로, 셔츠를 교환하는 것은 게임이 우호적이고 공정한 태도로 치러지고 있다는 것을 보여준다.

가장 유명한 유니폼 교환은 1970년 월드컵에서 브라질이 영국을 상대로 준준결승전에서 승리한 후에 일어났다. 브라질의 역대 최고 선수인 펠레는 영국의 역대 최고 선수인 보비 무어와 유니폼을 교환했다. 이 두 위대한 선수들이 셔츠를 교환하는 모습은 아마도 축구 역사에서 가장 유명한 장면일 것이다. 그때부터 펠레와 같은 유명한 축구 스타들은 다른 선수들보다 셔츠가 더 많이 필요했는데, 이는 상대 팀 선수들이 모두 그들과 셔츠를 교환하고 싶어 했기 때문이다.

오늘날, 유니폼 교환은 상대 선수들에게 우정과 존경을 보여주는 하나의 필수적인 부분으로서 모든 중요한 경기 후에 이루어진다. 사실, 이 때문에 선수들은 여분의 유니폼을 지급받고 있다!

어휘   whistle[hwísl] 몡 호각   intense[inténs] 톙 극심한; *치열한   jersey[dʒə́ːrzi] 몡 (운동 경기용) 셔츠
swap[swap] 통 바꾸다 몡 교환   opposing[əpóuziŋ] 톙 서로 겨루는   opponent[əpóunənt]
몡 (게임 · 대회 등의) 상대   spirit[spírit] 몡 정신; 태도   fair play 정정당당한 시합
medical[médikəl] 톙 의학의, 의료의   treatment[tríːtmənt] 몡 치료   likewise[láikwàiz]
튀 마찬가지로, 비슷하게   quarter-final[kwɔ̀ːrtərfáinl] 몡 준준결승   essential[isénʃəl] 톙 필수적인
respect[rispékt] 몡 존경   [문제] sportsmanship[spɔ́ːrtsmənʃip] 몡 스포츠맨 정신   switch[switʃ]
통 바꾸다   tackle[tǽkl] 몡 (축구의) 태클   significant[signífikənt] 톙 중요한

구문   1행   Someone [**watching** soccer for the first time] might be surprised by *what*
happens ....
• watching 이하는 Someone을 수식하는 현재분사구
• what: '…하는 것'의 의미로, 선행사를 포함하는 관계대명사

　　　4행   ... this has been a soccer tradition since 1931, **when** players from France and
England swapped shirts ....
• when: 1931을 보충 설명하는 계속적 용법의 관계부사

There are other similar traditions in soccer [**that** you *may have seen*].
- that 이하는 other similar traditions in soccer를 수식하는 목적격 관계대명사절
- may have v-ed: '…했을지도 모른다'라는 의미로, 과거 사실에 대한 불확실한 추측을 나타냄

10행 …, the ball is kicked out of play **so that** he or she **can** receive medical treatment.
- so that + 주어 + can …: ~가 …할 수 있도록

STRATEGIC SUMMARY important, helping, fairness, end, extra

EXPANDING KNOWLEDGE

1 d **2** *1)* F *2)* T

> 축구를 하기 위해 미국에 온 직후, 데이비드 베컴은 기자 회견을 했다. 회견 도중, 베컴은 미국에서 football을 하게 되어 기쁘다고 말했다. 이 말을 하고 나서, 그는 재빨리 정정해서 soccer라고 말했다. 왜 베컴은 이렇게 해야 했을까?
> 그의 모국인 영국에서 그가 하는 스포츠는 football이라고 불린다. 하지만 미국에서 데이비드 베컴의 스포츠는 soccer라고 불리며, football은 완전히 다른 스포츠를 가리키는 용어이다. 그렇다면 soccer라는 말은 어디에서 왔을까? 이는 그 스포츠의 옛 영국 이름인 'Association Football'의 일부였다. 사람들은 그것을 약식으로 'assoc'이라고 불렀고, 나중에 'as'를 빼고 'er'을 붙여 'soccer'를 만들어냈다. 그래서 많은 사람들이 'soccer'라는 말을 미국인들이 만들어냈다고 생각하지만, 그것은 사실상 영국 사람들에 의해 만들어졌다.

어휘 shortly[ʃɔ́ːrtli] ⑨ (시간상으로) 얼마 안 되어 press conference 기자 회견 correct[kərékt] ⑧ 바로잡다, 정정하다 term[təːrm] ⑨ 용어 entirely[intáiərli] ⑨ 완전히 association[əsòusiéiʃən] ⑨ 협회 informally[infɔ́ːrməli] ⑨ 비공식적으로, 약식으로 refer to …을 일컫다, 지칭하다 coin[kɔin] ⑧ (새로운 낱말·어구 등을) 만들다 [문제] differ[dífər] ⑧ 다르다

구문 3행 …, Beckham said that he was happy **to play** football in the United States.
- to play: 감정의 원인을 나타내는 부사적 용법의 to부정사

11행 People informally **referred to** it **as** "assoc" before [*dropping* "as"] and [*adding* "er"] **to form** "soccer."
- refer to A as B: A를 B라고 부르다
- dropping과 adding 이하는 전치사 before의 목적어 역할을 하는 동명사구
- to form: 결과를 나타내는 부사적 용법의 to부정사

VOCABULARY REVIEW

A 1 swap **2** fair **3** opponent **4** intense
B 1 refer to **2** correct **3** opposing **4** medical **5** extra **6** respect
C 1 b **2** c

unit 06 ANIMALS
pp. 28-31

Animal Behavior

1 b **2** c **3** d **4** b **5** Because they rely on each other for food and protection. **6** a

인간으로서 우리는 배려심 있고 너그러울 수 있지만, 이것이 우리를 다르게 하는 특징은 아니다. Linda Gustafson의 두 애완동물인 고양이 Toby와 개 Katie를 예로 들어보자. 매일 저녁, Gustafson 씨는 Toby와 Katie에게 저녁 식사 후 남은 음식을 먹이로 주곤 하는데, 반드시 Toby의 먹이를 Katie와는 멀리 떨어진 높은 선반에 올려 두곤 했다. 그러나 Toby는 Katie가 간청하면 불쌍히 여겨서 Katie가 더 먹을 수 있도록 약간의 먹이를 바닥으로 떼어 주곤 했다. 저녁 늦게 Katie는 마치 호의에 보답하듯이 쿠션 위의 자신의 아늑한 자리를 떠나 Toby가 거기 앉게 했다.

그러나 너그러움은 애완동물들에만 국한된 것이 아니다. 야생 생물학자인 Kayhan Ostovar는 사바나 코끼리 무리를 연구하던 중 같은 행동을 관찰했다. Ostovar에 따르면, 코에 심한 부상을 당한 낯선 숲 코끼리가 사바나 무리 중 한 코끼리에게 다가갔다. (동물 학대는 많은 동물 복지 협회에 의해 비난을 받고 반대된다.) 숲 코끼리는 즉시 더 큰 코끼리의 입에 코를 넣어서 스스로 먹이를 먹을 수 없다는 것을 알렸다. 본능적으로 사바나 코끼리는 약간의 음식을 집어 숲 코끼리의 입에 넣어주었다.

그렇다면 왜 일부 동물들은 그런 친절을 보이는 것일까? 과학자들은 그것이 집단 환경에서 사는 것과 관련이 있다고 생각한다. 집단 안에서 코끼리와 같은 동물들은 식량이나 방어를 위해 서로에게 의존한다. 그래서 그들은 집단의 다른 일원들과 좋은 관계를 유지해야 한다. 그러나 동물들은 때때로 뚜렷한 혜택을 얻을 수 없을 때조차 서로 돕는다. 아마 그들은 우리가 그러는 만큼 그저 선행을 베푸는 데서 오는 만족감을 즐기는 것일지도 모른다.

어휘　caring[kέəriŋ] 혱 배려하는, 보살피는　generous[dʒénərəs] 혱 너그러운, 관대한 (generosity 몡 너그러움, 관대함)　quality[kwɑ́ləti] 몡 특징　set ... apart …을 다르게[돋보이게] 만들다　feed[fiːd] 동 먹이를 주다　scrap[skræp] 몡 조각; *(pl.) 남은 음식　take pity on …을 불쌍히 여기다　beg[beg] 동 간청하다　scoop[skuːp] 동 퍼내다, 떠내다　cozy[kóuzi] 혱 아늑한　domestic[dəméstik] 혱 국내의; *애완용의　wildlife[wáildlàif] 몡 야생 동물　biologist[baiɑ́lədʒist] 몡 생물학자　observe[əbzə́ːrv] 동 관찰하다　behavior[bihéivjər] 몡 행동　herd[həːrd] 몡 떼, 무리　savannah[səvǽnə] 몡 사바나, 대초원　injured[índʒərd] 혱 부상당한　trunk[trʌŋk] 몡 (나무) 줄기; *(코끼리) 코　cruelty[krúːəlti] 몡 잔인함; *학대　criticize[krítəsàiz] 동 비난하다　instinctively[instíŋktivli] 부 본능적으로　rely on …에 의존하다　maintain[meintéin] 동 유지하다　obvious[ɑ́bviəs] 혱 뚜렷한, 명백한　benefit[bénəfit] 몡 혜택　satisfaction[sæ̀tisfǽkʃən] 몡 만족감
[문제] get along with …와 잘 지내다　favor[féivər] 몡 호의, 친절　drowning[dráuniŋ] 혱 물에 빠진　pack[pæk] 몡 짐; *(사냥개 · 이리 등의) 떼, 무리　hand over …을 넘겨주다

구문

3행　Every evening, Ms. Gustafson **would** feed Toby and Katie the scraps from her dinner, [*making* sure to put Toby's food …].
• would: '…하곤 했다'의 의미로, 과거의 반복된 행동을 나타냄
• making 이하는 동시동작을 나타내는 분사구문

6행　… he would scoop some food onto the floor **so that** Katie **could** eat more.
• so that + 주어 + can …: ~가 …할 수 있도록

7행　… cozy spot on the cushion and **let** Toby **sit** there, *as if* returning the favor.
• 사역동사(let) + 목적어 + 동사원형: …가 ~하게 하다
• as if: 마치 …인 것처럼

18행　Scientists think (that) it **has something to do with** living in a group environment.
• have something to do with: …와 관련이 있다

22행　…, animals sometimes help each other even when there is no obvious benefit **to be gained**.
• to be gained: no obvious benefit을 수식하는 형용사적 용법의 to부정사구

STRATEGIC SUMMARY　caring, return, injured, favor, enjoy

EXPANDING KNOWLEDGE

1 b　**2** *1)* T *2)* T

한때 피그미 침팬지라고 불렸던 보노보는 현재 다른 영장류보다 인간과 더 유사하다고 여겨진다.

예를 들어, 과학자들은 보노보가 우리와 가장 가까운 현존하는 동족이라고 믿는데, 유전학적으로 말하자면 보노보 DNA의 98퍼센트가 우리와 일치하기 때문이다. 호리호리한 상체와 어깨, 목, 긴 다리를 가진 보노보는 보통의 침팬지보다 외형적으로 인간을 더 비슷하게 닮았다. 사실, 보노보는 종종 두 다리로 서서 걷는다!

또한, 보노보의 행동도 우리와 비슷하다. 무리 지어 놀 때 보노보는 웃고 서로에게 간지럼을 태운다. 그리고 실험에서 그들은 인간 이외 동물계에서는 존재하지 않았던 동정심과 친절, 인내심, 협동의 능력을 보여주었다. 그들은 과제를 수행하기 위해 도구를 사용하기까지 한다! 이 정도로 분명하게 동물에 반영된 우리 자신을 보다니 놀랍지 않은가?

어휘 primate[práimeit] 몡 영장류 relative[rélətiv] 몡 친척; *동족 genetically[dʒənétikəli] 뮈 유전적으로 identical[aidéntikəl] 혱 동일한, 일치하는 slender[sléndər] 혱 호리호리한 resemble[rizémbl] 동 닮다 tickle[tíkl] 동 간지럼을 태우다 experiment[ikspérəmənt] 몡 실험 demonstrate[démənstrèit] 동 보여주다 capacity[kəpǽsəti] 몡 능력 compassion[kəmpǽʃən] 몡 동정심 patience[péiʃəns] 몡 인내심 cooperation[kouὰpəréiʃən] 몡 협동 unknown[ʌnnóun] 혱 알려지지 않은; *발생한 적이 없는 animal kingdom 동물계 accomplish[əkámpliʃ] 동 완수하다 task[tæsk] 몡 과제 reflect[riflékt] 동 반영하다, 나타내다

구문 11행 Isn't **it** amazing [**to see** ourselves *reflected* so clearly in an animal]?
- it은 가주어이고, to see 이하가 진주어
- see(지각동사) + 목적어 + v-ed: '…가 ~되는 것을 보다'라는 의미로, 목적어와 목적격보어가 수동 관계일 때 과거분사를 씀

VOCABULARY REVIEW

A **1** slender **2** domestic **3** primate **4** compassion
B **1** genetically **2** generosity **3** took pity on **4** caring **5** tickling **6** instinctively
C **1** d **2** a

07 PLACES

pp. 32-35

Special Dining

1 c **2** b **3** d **4** b **5** They can enter with their right hand on the shoulder of the person in front of them. **6** b

거의 무한한 시각 정보가 있는 세상에서, 때때로 그냥 눈을 감고 심호흡을 해보는 것은 중요합니다. 어서 지금 그것을 해보세요. 말씀해 보세요. 무슨 냄새가 나요? 무슨 소리가 들리나요? 무엇이 느껴지나요? 시각을 차단함으로써, 우리는 다른 감각들을 강화할 수 있습니다. 이것이 Opaque 배후에 있는 생각, 즉 전국을 휩쓸고 있는 '어둠 속에서 식사하기' 경험입니다.

Opaque는 단순한 음식점 그 이상으로, 그것은 식사하는 새로운 방법입니다. Opaque에 들어가자마자, 여러분은 조명이 밝은 라운지에서 저희 직원들의 환영을 받을 것입니다. (인사는 서비스업에서 핵심 전략입니다.) 여러분이 식사와 음료를 주문할 곳이 바로 여기입니다. 그리고 저희 직원에게 여러분의 코트와 가방을 맡길 것을 기억해주세요. 어둠 속에서는 그것들이 필요하지 않을 것입니다.

일단 여유가 생기고 준비가 되면, 여러분과 일행의 다른 구성원들은 식당으로 안내될 것입니다. 여러분 앞에 있는 사람의 어깨에 오른손을 얹고, 여러분은 새로운 느낌의 식사를 위해 어둠으로 들어갈 것입니다. 저희 식당 웨이터들은 모두 여러분이 식사 경험을 최대로 즐기도록 도울 수 있게 교육받은 시각장애인입니다. 시각이 없어도, 단순한 식사 행위는 근본적으로 더 즐거워질 것입니다. 냄새는 훨씬 더 강해지고 풍미는 훨씬 더 깊어질 것입니다.

비평가들과 손님들 모두 Opaque에서의 '어둠 속에서 식사하기' 경험을 칭찬하고 있습니다. 만약 여러분이 다른 어떤 것과도 같지 않은 식사 경험을 원하신다면, 오늘 예약하세요. 어둠 속에서 저희와 함께하세요. Opaque에서 저희와 함께하세요.

어휘 limitless[límitlis] 혤 무한한　visual[víʒuəl] 혤 시각의　strengthen[stréŋkθən] 통 강화하다　dining[dáiniŋ] 몡 식사 (dine 통 식사하다)　sweep[swi:p] 통 쓸다; *급속히 퍼지다[휩쓸다]　party[pá:rti] 몡 파티; *단체, 일행　sensation[senséiʃən] 몡 느낌, 감각　handicapped[hǽndikæpt] 혤 장애를 가진　to the fullest 최대한도로　sight[sait] 몡 시각　radically[rǽdikəli] 틧 근본적으로　critic[krítik] 몡 비평가, 평론가　alike[əláik] 틧 둘 다, 똑같이　make a reservation 예약하다　[문제] modernize[mádərnàiz] 통 현대화하다　boost[bu:st] 통 신장시키다, 북돋우다　advertise[ǽdvərtàiz] 통 광고하다　enhance[inhǽns] 통 향상하다　cut off 중단시키다, 차단하다　keen[ki:n] 혤 예민한, 예리한

구문　9행　**Upon entering** Opaque, you will be greeted by our staff ....
　　　　　　• upon v-ing: …하자마자 곧
　　　　11행　**It is** here **that** you will order your meal and drinks.
　　　　　　• It is ... that ~: '~한 것은 바로 …이다'의 의미로, here을 강조하는 강조구문
　　　　16행　**With** your right hand (being) **on** the shoulder of the person in front of you, ...
　　　　　　• with + 명사 + v-ing: '…가 ~한 채로'라는 의미의 분사구문으로, on 앞에 현재분사 being이 생략되어 있음
　　　　18행　... are all visually handicapped people [**who** are trained to *help* you *enjoy* your dining experience ...].
　　　　　　• who 이하는 visually handicapped people을 수식하는 주격 관계대명사절
　　　　　　• help + 목적어 + 동사원형: …가 ~하도록 돕다
　　　　20행　Smells will become **much** stronger and *flavors* (will become) **much** richer.
　　　　　　• much: '훨씬'의 의미로, 비교급을 수식하는 부사
　　　　　　• flavors 뒤에 반복되는 부분인 will become이 생략되어 있음

STRATEGIC SUMMARY stronger, unique, shoulder, visual, richer

EXPANDING KNOWLEDGE

1 a　**2** *1)* T　*2)* F

나는 먹는 것이 어려울 수 있다고 생각해본 적이 없지만, Opaque를 방문하고 나서 그것이 얼마나 어려울 수 있는지 깨닫게 되었다. 식사를 받았을 때, 나는 아무것도 볼 수 없었다. 오직 내 음식 냄새만 맡을 수 있었다. 처음에는 나이프와 포크를 사용했지만, 곧 손으로 먹는 것이 더 쉽다는 것을 알아차렸다. 어쨌든, 아무도 나를 볼 수 없었다. 한편, 나의 다른 모든 감각이 더 강해진 것 같았다. 예를 들어, 나는 다른 식탁의 사람들이 이야기하는 것을 쉽게 들었다. 심지어 소금 한 톨을 맛볼 수도 있을 것처럼 느껴졌다. 무엇보다도 어둠 속에서 식사하는 것은 안 보이는 것이 얼마나 힘든지를 이해할 수 있게 해주었고, 내가 <u>볼 수 있어서</u> 얼마나 운이 좋은지에 대해 감사하게 해주었다.

어휘 meanwhile[mí:nwàil] 틧 그동안에; *한편　grain[grein] 몡 곡물; *(특정 물질의) 알갱이　blind[blaind] 혤 눈이 먼, 맹인인　appreciate[əprí:ʃièit] 통 진가를 알아보다; *고마워하다

구문　3행　..., but soon I realized that **it** was easier [**to eat** with my hands].
　　　　　　• it은 가주어이고, to eat 이하가 진주어

7행 …, dining in the dark **allowed** me **to understand** [*how* difficult it is to be blind] and **made** me **appreciate** [*how* lucky I am to be able to see].

- allow + 목적어 + to-v: …가 ~하게 하다
- how 이하는 각각 동사 understand와 appreciate의 목적어 역할을 하는 간접의문문
- 사역동사(make) + 목적어 + 동사원형: …가 ~하게 하다

VOCABULARY REVIEW

A **1** relaxed **2** sweep **3** praise **4** limitless
B **1** strategy **2** appreciate **3** critic **4** reservation **5** radically **6** handicapped
C **1** b **2** c

unit 08 HISTORY

pp. 36-39

Napoleon

1 a **2** d **3** b **4** Because they were much bigger than normal people, and they wore hats with tall crowns. **5** c **6** *1)* T *2)* F

> 때때로 유난히 키가 작고 공격적인 남자는 '나폴레옹 콤플렉스'가 있다고 한다. 이것은 19세기 초반 유럽의 많은 지역을 정복했던 유명한 프랑스 장군 나폴레옹이 매우 키가 작았다는 생각에 근거한다. 그러나 새로운 증거는 나폴레옹이 특별히 작지 않았음을 시사한다. 그렇다면, 왜 그의 키에 대한 이런 이야기가 생긴 것일까?
>
> 한 가지 이유는 프랑스와 영국에서 사람들이 키를 측정했던 방법과 관련이 있었다. 양국 모두에서 키를 측정하기 위해 피트와 인치가 사용되었지만, 프랑스식과 영국식의 치수는 같지 않았다. 프랑스에서는 1인치가 2.71cm인 반면, 영국에서는 1인치가 겨우 2.41cm였다. 그래서 나폴레옹이 5피트 2인치라고 묘사되었을 때, 영국인들은 이것이 그가 평균보다 더 작다는 것을 의미한다고 생각했다. 그러나 이는 영국 단위로는 5피트 6.5인치에 해당하는데, 이는 그가 실제로는 평균적인 프랑스인보다 더 컸다는 것을 의미한다!
>
> 나폴레옹의 키 이야기에 대한 또 다른 이유는 경호원들 옆에 서는 그의 습관 때문이었다. 그의 경호원들은 일반인보다 훨씬 더 커서 나폴레옹이 상대적으로 작아 보였다. 게다가 나폴레옹은 꼭대기가 낮은 모자를 썼던 반면, 경호원들은 꼭대기가 높은 모자를 썼다. 다른 모자가 나폴레옹을 훨씬 더 작아 보이게 했다.
>
> 오늘날 많은 사람들이 이 오해에 대해 알고 있지만, 나폴레옹은 여전히 키가 작은 남자의 상징이다. 왜 그럴까? 그것은 그의 키가 1800년대 초반부터 영국 문화의 아주 중요한 부분이 되었기 때문인데, 이때에는 영국과 프랑스가 적이었다. 영국인들은 프랑스인들을 무시하는 방편으로 나폴레옹을 종종 조롱했고, 따라서 나폴레옹의 키에 관한 농담이 아주 유명해졌다. 이것이 그가 키가 작은 남자였다는 이야기가 오늘날 여전히 남아있는 이유이다.

어휘 aggressive [əgrésiv] 형 공격적인 complex [kámpleks] 명 콤플렉스, 강박 관념 general [dʒénərəl] 명 장군 conquer [káŋkər] 동 정복하다 evidence [évədəns] 명 증거 myth [miθ] 명 신화; *(근거 없는) 이야기 measure [méʒər] 동 측정하다 (measurement 명 측정; *치수) height [hait] 명 키, 신장 average [ǽvəridʒ] 명 평균 형 평균의 correspond [kɔ̀:rəspánd] 동 일치하다; *해당하다 bodyguard [bádigà:rd] 명 보디가드, 경호원 normal [nɔ́:rməl] 형 보통의 in comparison 비교해 보면 crown [kraun] 명 왕관; *(모자의) 정수리[꼭대기] misconception [mìskənsépʃən] 명 오해 [문제] make up for 만회하다 fight off …와 싸워 물리치다 look up to …을 존경하다 look down on …을 얕보다

구문 2행 This is based on the idea [**that** the famous French general Napoleon, …].
- that: the idea와 동격인 명사절을 이끄는 접속사

14

9행 So, when Napoleon was **described as** [*being* 5 feet 2 inches], ...
- describe A as B: A를 B로 묘사하다
- being 이하는 전치사 as의 목적어 역할을 하는 동명사구

10행 But this corresponds to 5 feet 6.5 inches in English terms, **which** means he ....
- which: 앞의 절을 선행사로 하는 계속적 용법의 주격 관계대명사

17행 The different hats **made** Napoleon **seem** *even* shorter.
- 사역동사(make) + 목적어 + 동사원형: …가 ~하게 하다
- even: '훨씬'의 의미로, 비교급을 강조하는 부사

20행 … such an important part of British culture from the early 1800s, **when** Britain and France were enemies.
- when: the early 1800s를 보충 설명하는 계속적 용법의 관계부사

STRATEGIC ORGANIZER Misconceptions, different, large, shorter, rivalry

EXPANDING KNOWLEDGE

1 d **2** *1)* F *2)* T

1804년에 나폴레옹은 민법전이라고도 알려진 나폴레옹 법전을 도입했다. 나폴레옹 법전은 유럽 전역에 통일되고 논리적인 법체계를 만들어냈다.

새 법의 대부분은 유익했지만, 모든 사람이 그 법으로부터 혜택을 받은 것은 아니었다. 민법전은 여성들의 많은 자유를 제한했다. 예를 들어, 여성은 남편의 허락 없이는 재산을 사거나 팔 수 없었다. 민법전은 또한 이혼법을 강화했고 남편을 가정의 지배자로 만들었다. 반면에, 민법전은 여러 면에서 진보적이었다. 이 때문에 결과적으로 대륙 전역에 운하, 항구, 개선된 도로를 만드는 공공사업의 체계가 만들어졌다. 교육 제도 역시 혜택을 받았는데, 이것으로 사립 학교가 생겨났으며, 글을 읽고 쓸 줄 아는 능력이 보다 중시되었다.

나폴레옹 법전은 오늘날에도 여전히 영향력을 발휘하며 나폴레옹의 가장 큰 유산으로 남아 있다.

어휘 introduce[ìntrədjúːs] ⑧ 도입하다 civil code 민법전 unified[júːnifàid] ⑲ 통일된 logical[ládʒikəl] ⑲ 논리적인 property[prápərti] ⑲ 재산 permission[pərmíʃən] ⑲ 허락 divorce[divɔ́ːrs] ⑲ 이혼 ruler[rúːlər] ⑲ 지배자 progressive[prəgrésiv] ⑲ 진보적인 result in (결과적으로) …을 낳다[야기하다] canal[kənǽl] ⑲ 운하 harbor[háːrbər] ⑲ 항구 emphasis[émfəsis] ⑲ 강조 literacy[lítərəsi] ⑲ 글을 읽고 쓰는 능력 influential[influénʃəl] ⑲ 영향력이 있는 legacy[légəsi] ⑲ 유산 [문제] weaken[wíːkən] ⑧ 약화하다

구문 1행 …, Napoleon introduced the Napoleonic Code, (which is) **also known as** the Civil Code.
- also known as 앞에 '주격 관계대명사 + be동사'가 생략되어 있음

9행 It resulted in a system of public works [**that** created canals, harbors, …].
- that 이하는 a system of public works를 수식하는 주격 관계대명사절

11행 The educational system also benefited, **which** resulted in ….
- which: 앞의 절을 선행사로 하는 계속적 용법의 주격 관계대명사

VOCABULARY REVIEW

A 1 logical **2** myth **3** aggressive **4** permission
B 1 introduce **2** misconception **3** Literacy **4** unified **5** average **6** strengthen
C 1 c **2** d

★Alice's Adventures in Wonderland

1 b   **2** Because it seemed to be talking to itself and it was wearing a watch.   **3** d   **4** a   **5** b
6 *1)* F *2)* F

> 앨리스는 언니와 함께 강가에 앉아 있었고 몹시 지루해하고 있었다. 언니는 책을 읽고 있었지만, 앨리스는 할 일이 없었다. 그녀가 야생화를 좀 꺾을까 생각하고 있을 때 하얀 토끼가 달려가는 것을 보았다. 토끼를 보는 것은 이상할 게 없었다. 강 근처에는 많은 토끼가 살고 있었다. 그러나 이 토끼는 혼잣말을 하고 있는 것 같았다! 계속해서 "아 이런! 늦겠어!"라고 말하고 있었다. 그러고 나서 토끼는 멈춰서 자신의 시계를 보더니 서둘러 갔다.
>
> 이제야 이 광경은 아주 이상했다. 앨리스는 전에 시계를 찬 토끼를 본 적이 없었다. 호기심에 그녀는 자리에서 일어나 토끼를 따라가기 시작했다. 그녀는 들판을 지나 뒤쫓아 가다가 토끼가 커다란 구멍으로 뛰어내리는 것을 보았다. 주저하지 않고 앨리스는 토끼를 따라 구멍으로 내려갔다. 그녀가 멈춰 생각했더라면, 어떻게 돌아 나올지 생각했을 것이다. 그러나 대신 그녀는 바로 뛰어들어 떨어지기 시작했다.
>
> 구멍이 매우 깊거나 아니면 앨리스가 아주 <u>천천히</u> 떨어지고 있었다. 다음에 무슨 일이 벌어질지 생각할 시간이 넉넉했다. 그녀는 아래를 보려고 했지만, 너무 어두워서 아무것도 볼 수 없었다. '얼마나 깊이 떨어졌을지 궁금해'라고 그녀는 생각했다. 수 마일 아래로, 아래로, 아래로 내려가는 것 같았다. 낙하가 절대 끝나지 않을 것 같았! '지구의 중심에 가까워지고 있는 게 틀림없어'라고 그녀는 생각했다. '지구를 뚫고 떨어지게 되려나! 머리를 아래로 하고 걷는 사람들 사이로 나오게 되면 얼마나 재미있을까!' 그리고 그때, 갑자기, 그녀는 쿵 하는 소리와 함께 마른 잎 더미로 떨어졌다. 낙하가 마침내 다 끝난 것이다!

어휘   adventure[ædvéntʃər] 몡 모험   terribly[térəbli] 뿐 몹시   wildflower[wáildflàuər] 몡 야생화
talk to oneself 혼잣말을 하다   hurry on 서두르다, 급히 가다   curious[kjúəriəs] 혱 궁금한,
호기심이 많은   chase[tʃeis] 통 뒤쫓다   hesitate[hézətèit] 통 주저하다   fall[fɔːl] 통 떨어지다
몡 낙하   downward[dáunwərd] 뿐 아래로   land[lænd] 통 착륙하다   thump[θʌmp] 몡 쿵 하는
소리   pile[pail] 몡 더미

구문   9행   Alice **had** never **seen** a rabbit [*wearing* a watch] before.
　　　　　　• had seen: 과거 기준 시점까지의 경험을 나타내는 과거완료
　　　　　　• wearing 이하는 a rabbit을 수식하는 현재분사구
　　12행   **If** she **had stopped** to think, she **might have wondered** [*how* she would get back out].
　　　　　　• If + 주어 + had v-ed, 주어 + 조동사의 과거형 + have v-ed: 가정법 과거완료
　　　　　　• how 이하는 동사 wondered의 목적어 역할을 하는 간접의문문
　　15행   **Either** the hole was very deep **or** Alice was falling very slowly.
　　　　　　• either A or B: A와 B 둘 중 하나
　　16행   She had a lot of time **to wonder** what would happen next.
　　　　　　• to wonder: a lot of time을 수식하는 형용사적 용법의 to부정사

STRATEGIC SUMMARY   bored, ordinary, curious, lasted, landed

EXPANDING KNOWLEDGE

1 a   **2** a

루이스 캐럴의 *이상한 나라의 앨리스*는 토끼 굴로 떨어져서 기이한 상상의 생명체들로 가득한 환상의 나라에 있는 자신을 발견하게 되는 앨리스라는 이름의 소녀에 관한 것이다. 이야기는 순전히 허구처럼 들리지만, 사실은 현실의 삶에서 영감을 받았다.

　　1856년에 캐럴은 Lorina와 Alice, Edith라는 이름의 세 자매와 친구가 되었다. 다음 몇 해 동안 그는 그 소녀들과 많은 시간을 보냈고 그들을 즐겁게 해줄 이야기를 만들어냈다. 한 이야기가 Alice라는 소녀와 그녀가 지하 세계에서 겪은 환상적인 모험에 관한 것이었다. Lorina와 Edith 역시 그 이야기에 등장했다. Alice는 그 이야기를 아주 좋아해서 캐럴에게 글로 써달라고 부탁했다. 원고를 출판하기 전에, 캐럴은 삽화가 John Tenniel에게 책의 그림을 그리게 했다.

　　*이상한 나라의 앨리스*는 단숨에 성공했다. 오늘날 그것은 125개의 언어로 번역되었고 아이와 어른들 모두가 매우 좋아하는 이야기로 남아있다.

어휘　fantasy[fǽntəsi] 명 공상, 환상 (fantastic 형 환상적인)　imaginary[imǽdʒənèri] 형 상상의 creature[kríːtʃər] 명 생명체　pure[pjuər] 형 순수한; *완전한, 순전한　fiction[fíkʃən] 명 소설; *허구 inspire[inspáiər] 동 영감을 주다　make up 지어내다, 만들어내다　entertain[èntərtéin] 동 즐겁게 하다　underground[ʌ̀ndərgráund] 부 지하에서　publish[pʌ́bliʃ] 동 출판하다　script[skript] 명 원고　illustrator[íləstrèitər] 명 삽화가　instant[ínstənt] 형 즉각적인　translate[trænsléit] 동 번역하다　tale[teil] 명 이야기

구문　7행　One was about a girl [**named** Alice] and the fantastic adventures [(which[that]) *she had* underground].
　　　　• named 이하는 a girl을 수식하는 과거분사구
　　　　• she had 앞에 the fantastic adventures를 선행사로 하는 목적격 관계대명사가 생략되어 있음
　　10행　..., Carroll **had** illustrator John Tenniel **draw** pictures for the book.
　　　　• 사역동사(have) + 목적어 + 동사원형: …가 ~하게 하다

VOCABULARY REVIEW
A　*1* translate　*2* illustrator　*3* instant　*4* hesitate
B　*1* terribly　*2* inspired　*3* fiction　*4* curious　*5* underground　*6* creature
C　*1* d　*2* b

unit
10 PSYCHOLOGY　pp. 44-47

Handwriting
1 d　**2** d　**3** The person might be shy.　**4** c　**5** d　**6** *1)* T　*2)* F

지문 외에, 우리를 개개인으로 구별해주는 것에는 무엇이 있을까? 우리의 필체가 그러한 역할을 한다는 사실을 알면 놀랄지도 모른다. 모든 사람에게는 그들의 성격을 반영하는 고유한 필체가 있다. 중국의 위대한 철학자인 공자는 '바람 속의 갈대와 같이 흔들리는 필체를 가진 사람을 주의하라.'라는 말로 이러한 생각을 드러냈다.

　　당신은 필적을 조사하는 것만으로 어떤 사람의 성격에 대해 많은 것을 알아낼 수 있다. 예를 들어, 필체가 단정한 사람은 대체로 믿을 만하지만, 필체가 엉망인 사람은 비밀이 많다. 작은 글씨는 그 사람이 수줍음이 많을 수도 있음을 의미하는 <u>반면</u>, 큰 글씨는 그 사람이 주목받기 좋아한다는 것을 나타낸다. 필체 분석가들은 또한 연결성을 살핀다. 글자들이 연결되어 있으면, 그 사람은 조심성이 많을 것이지만, 글자 사이에 간격이 있으면, 그 사람은 예술적일 것이다.

필체 분석은 실질적인 쓰임이 많다. 예를 들어, 경찰은 때때로 용의자의 원래 필적과 위조문서를 비교하기 위해 필체 분석가를 고용한다. 분석가들은 용의자가 범죄를 저질렀는지 알아내기 위해 두 가지 표본 사이의 주된 차이점을 찾는다. 많은 회사들도 채용 여부를 결정할 때 필체 분석가를 고용한다. 분석가들은 지원자들의 개인적인 특성을 더 알아내기 위해 그들의 필체를 확인한다. 어떤 사람들은 심지어 필체 요법이라고 알려진 과정을 통해 개인의 나쁜 습관과 특성을 바꾸는 데 필체 분석이 사용될 수 있다고 말한다.

그러나 필체 분석에는 한계가 있음을 인식하는 것이 중요하다. 분석가들은 개인의 나이나 인종, 성별, 심지어 그들이 왼손잡이인지 오른손잡이인지도 구별할 수 없다. 그럼에도 불구하고, 필체는 여러 상황에서 사람들에 관한 흥미로운 정보를 드러낼 수 있다. 그러므로 다음번에 누군가의 필체를 볼 때는 그 사람의 성격이 어떤지 추측해보라.

어휘 fingerprint[fíŋgərprìnt] 몡 지문   distinguish[distíŋgwiʃ] 통 구별하다   handwriting[hǽndràitiŋ] 몡 필체, 필적   reflect[riflékt] 통 반영하다   personality[pə̀rsənǽləti] 몡 성격   philosopher[filásəfər] 몡 철학자   beware of …을 주의하다   sway[swei] 통 흔들리다   reed[ri:d] 몡 갈대   neat[ni:t] 혱 단정한   reliable[riláiəbl] 혱 믿을 만한   messy[mési] 혱 엉망인   secretive[sí:kritiv] 혱 비밀스러운   indicate[índikèit] 통 나타내다   analyst[ǽnəlist] 몡 분석가 (analysis 몡 분석)   cautious[kɔ́:ʃəs] 혱 조심성이 있는   employ[implɔ́i] 통 고용하다   suspect[sʌ́spekt] 몡 용의자   forge[fɔ:rdʒ] 통 구축하다; *위조하다   document[dάkjumənt] 몡 문서   commit[kəmít] 통 (범죄를) 저지르다   trait[treit] 몡 (성격상의) 특성   limitation[lìmətéiʃən] 몡 한계(점)   gender[dʒéndər] 몡 성별   reveal[rivíːl] 통 드러내다   [문제] consequently [kάnsəkwèntli] 튀 따라서   investigate[invéstəgèit] 통 조사하다   identify[aidéntəfài] 통 (신원 등을) 확인하다

구문 5행   Beware of a man [**whose** handwriting sways like reeds in the wind].
　　　　　　• whose 이하는 a man을 수식하는 소유격 관계대명사절
　　　17행   The analysts look for major differences between the two samples **to determine** [*whether* the suspect committed the crime].
　　　　　　• to determine: '…하기 위해'라는 의미로, 목적을 나타내는 부사적 용법의 to부정사
　　　　　　• whether: '…인지 (아닌지)'의 의미로, 동사 determine의 목적어인 명사절을 이끄는 접속사
　　　19행   Many companies also employ handwriting analysts [**when making** hiring decisions].
　　　　　　• when making 이하는 때를 나타내는 분사구문으로, 의미를 명확히 하기 위해 접속사를 생략하지 않음
　　　21행   … handwriting analysis can **be used to change** a person's bad habits and traits through a process [*known* as handwriting therapy].
　　　　　　• be used to-v: …하는 데 사용되다
　　　　　　• known 이하는 a process를 수식하는 과거분사구

STRATEGIC ORGANIZER personality, shyness, Practical, companies, therapy

EXPANDING KNOWLEDGE

1 b   **2** *1)* T *2)* F

필적 요법에 따르면 사람들이 필체를 바꿈으로써 그들의 성격을 개선할 수 있다고 한다. 그러나 어떻게 그것이 가능할까?

당신이 글씨를 쓸 때, 그것은 리듬과 속도, 압력, 방향을 사용하는 일련의 움직임을 수반한다. 이들 움직임은 가장 깊은 곳에 내재된 느낌과 감정에 의해 영향을 받는다. 그래서 필체는 신체적, 정신적, 감정적인 상태를 반영한다. 이것은 모두가 정해진 방식에 따라 쓰는 법을 배우는데도 불구하고 왜 저마다 고유한 필체를 갖는지를 설명해준다. 사실 한 과학자는 두 사람이 정확히 같은 필체를 가질 가능성은 68조 분의 1이라고 계산했다.

필적 요법은 아이들에게 가장 효과적이라고 하는데, 이는 아이들이 아직 필체와 성격을 형성해가는 중이기 때문이다. 그러나 아주 고집스러운 성인일지라도 긍정적인 변화를 보는 것이 가능할지도 모른다.

어휘 graphotherapy[ɡrǽfəθérəpi] 몡 필적 요법 manual[mǽnjuəl] 뤵 손으로 하는 pressure[préʃər] 몡 압력 mental[méntl] 뤵 정신적인 established[istǽbliʃt] 뤵 자리를 잡은, 확립된 calculate[kǽlkjulèit] 됭 계산하다 possibility[pàsəbíləti] 몡 가능성 trillion[tríljən] 몡 1조 [문제] alter[ɔ́ːltər] 됭 바꾸다 chance[tʃǽns] 몡 기회; *가능성

구문 7행 This explains (the reason) **why** each person has a unique way of writing, even though everybody learns *how to write* ....
  • why: 이유를 나타내는 관계부사로, 앞에 선행사 the reason이 생략되어 있음
  • how to-v: …하는 방법

9행 ... the possibility of **two people** [*having* the exact same handwriting] is **one in 68 trillion**.
  • two people: 동명사의 의미상 주어
  • having 이하는 전치사 of의 목적어 역할을 하는 동명사구
  • one in + 숫자: … 중에 하나

VOCABULARY REVIEW

A **1** sway **2** manual **3** forge **4** suspect
B **1** beware of **2** trait **3** applicants **4** reveal **5** stubborn **6** messy
C **1** b **2** a

unit **11 ECONOMY**

pp. 48-51

Odd Pricing

1 b **2** b **3** c **4** compete with their larger rivals **5** b **6** 1) F 2) F

우리는 종종 어떤 상품에 대해 10달러가 아닌 9.99달러를 지불한다. 왜 그렇게 많은 가격이 99와 같은 홀수로 끝나는 것일까? 몇 가지 이론이 있다.

가장 잘 알려진 이론은 *시카고 데일리 뉴스*와 관련이 있다. 1870년대에 그 회사의 소유주인 Melville E. Stone은 시카고에 필요한 것이 그 당시 판매되던 5센트짜리 신문과 경쟁할 1센트짜리 신문이라고 판단했다. 하지만 문제가 있었는데, 대부분의 상품이 소비자의 편의를 위해 짝수로 가격이 매겨져 있어서, 쓸 수 있는 1센트짜리가 많지 않았다. 1센트짜리를 더 많이 유통시키기 위해 그는 상점 주인들에게 가격을 약간만 낮춰달라고 설득했다. 그는 상품이 1달러가 아니라 '단' 99센트라면 소비자들이 상품을 구매할 가능성이 더 클 것이라고 말했고, 그가 옳았다. 곧 사람들이 *데일리 뉴스*를 살 수 있는 1센트짜리가 더 많이 생겼고 신문 판매 부수도 증가했다.

그러나 오늘날 거의 모든 가격을 홀수로 끝나게 하는 관행에 대한 더 그럴듯한 설명이 있다. 경제 호황기였던 1880년대에 미국 소매 시장은 고도의 경쟁을 겪었다. 더 큰 경쟁 상대들과 겨루기 위해, 시카고의 소규모 회사들은 '바로 아래의' 가격을 사용하기 시작했다. 예를 들어, 그들은 경쟁사들이 2달러에 판매하는 제품을 1.99달러로 광고했다. 그러한 가격 전략은 소비자들에게 큰 심리적 영향을 끼쳐 그 상품들이 더 저렴해 보이게 만들었다.

시카고의 소규모 사업체들에서 비롯된 상품 가격을 홀수로 매기는 관행은 세계적으로 보편적인 전략으로 발전했다. 당신이 구입하고 싶은 것이 무엇이든, 세계 어느 곳에 있든, 홀수 가격이라는 심리적 속임수는 아마도 당신이 구매하도록 설득하는 데 이용될 것이다.

어휘
price[prais] 명 값, 가격 동 값[가격]을 매기다   odd[ad] 형 이상한; *홀수의   penny[péni] 명 (영)
페니; *(미) 센트   compete[kəmpíːt] 동 경쟁하다 (competition 명 경쟁)   nickel[níkəl] 명 니켈;
*(미) 5센트   even[íːvən] 형 평평한; *짝수의   figure[fígjər] 명 숫자   convenience[kənvíːnjəns]
명 편의   spare[spɛər] 동 (시간·돈 등을) 할애하다[내주다]   circulation[sə̀ːrkjuléiʃən] 명 유통;
(신문의) 판매 부수   slightly[sláitli] 부 약간, 조금   purchase[pə́ːrtʃəs] 동 구매하다 명 구매
custom[kʌ́stəm] 명 관습   boom[buːm] 명 (경제의) 호황   retail market 소매 시장
strategy[strǽtədʒi] 명 전략   psychological[sàikəládʒikəl] 형 심리적인   practice[prǽktis]
명 실천; *관행   evolve[iválv] 동 발달하다   tactic[tǽktik] 명 전략   trick[trik] 명 속임수
[문제] in stock 비축되어, 재고로   get over …을 극복하다   adopt[ədápt] 동 입양하다; *(방법·자세
등을) 쓰다[취하다]   volume[váljuːm] 명 대량   sector[séktər] 명 분야

구문
8행   ... **what** Chicago needed was a penny newspaper *to compete* with the nickel
papers [**that** were available at the time].
• what: '…하는 것'의 의미로, 선행사를 포함하는 관계대명사(= the thing which)
• to compete: a penny newspaper를 수식하는 형용사적 용법의 to부정사
• that 이하는 the nickel papers를 수식하는 주격 관계대명사절

11행   ...: **with** most goods **priced** at even figures for the convenience of shoppers, ...
• with + 명사 + v-ed: '…가 ~된 채로'라는 의미의 분사구문으로, 명사와 분사가 수동 관계일 때
과거분사를 씀

19행   ..., there is a more likely explanation for today's custom of [**having** nearly every
price *end* in odd numbers].
• having 이하는 전치사 of의 목적어 역할을 하는 동명사구
• 사역동사(have) + 목적어 + 동사원형: …가 ~하게 하다

24행   ... a powerful psychological effect on customers, [**making** the products *appear*
cheaper].
• making 이하는 동시동작을 나타내는 분사구문
• 사역동사(make) + 목적어 + 동사원형: …가 ~하게 하다

29행   **Whatever** you're interested in purchasing, *wherever* you are in the world, ...
• whatever: '무엇을 …하더라도'라는 의미의 복합관계대명사(= no matter what)
• wherever: '어디에서 …하더라도'라는 의미의 복합관계부사(= no matter where)

STRATEGIC SUMMARY   end, worried, lower, compete, odd

EXPANDING KNOWLEDGE

1 d **2** c

가격은 단순한 숫자 그 이상이다. 그것은 쇼핑객에게 강한 심리적 영향을 미칠 수 있다. 예를 들어, 높은 가격은
설령 그렇지 않더라도 상품의 품질이 높다고 믿게 할 수 있다. 또한, 9.99달러처럼 홀수로 끝나는 가격은 9.99달러가
10달러보다 단 1센트 적을 뿐인데도 상품의 가격이 괜찮다는 인상을 만들어낸다. 이러한 기법은 상품의 가격이
100달러에서 199달러 사이처럼 가격대로 분류될 때 특히 강력하다. 이러한 경우에, 199달러로 가격이 매겨진 상품은
200달러짜리 상품보다 더 낮은 가격대에 나타날 것이다. 이것은 그 상품이 훨씬 더 저렴한 것처럼 보이게 한다.
그러므로 현명한 소비자가 되고 싶다면, 구매하기 전에 상품이나 서비스의 가격에 대해 신중하게 생각하라. 가격이
보이는 것만큼 좋지 않을지도 모른다.

어휘
impression[impréʃən] 명 인상   deal[diːl] 명 거래   particularly[pərtíkjulərli] 부 특히
range[reindʒ] 명 (범위 등을 일정하게 나눈) 대   [문제] behavioral[bihéivjərəl] 형 행동의
associate[əsóuʃièit] 동 연관 짓다   bargain[báːrgən] 명 싼 물건, 특가품

구문
4행   Also, prices [**that** end in odd numbers, such as $9.99], create an impression [*that*
a product is a good deal], ...

- that 이하는 prices를 수식하는 주격 관계대명사절
- that: an impression과 동격인 명사절을 이끄는 접속사

9행 In this case, a product [**priced** $199] would appear in a lower price range than a product [*costing* $200].
- priced 이하는 바로 앞의 a product를 수식하는 과거분사구
- costing 이하는 바로 앞의 a product를 수식하는 현재분사구

VOCABULARY REVIEW

A *1* psychological *2* evolve *3* theory *4* retail
B *1* impression *2* slightly *3* competition *4* deal *5* persuade *6* boom
C *1* b *2* c

unit 12 HERITAGE

pp. 52-55

Art Preservation

1 b *2* c *3* d *4* a *5* maintain a work of art's original features *6* *1)* T *2)* F

로댕의 *생각하는 사람*, 미켈란젤로의 시스티나 성당 천장화, 캄보디아의 앙코르와트, 그리고 수천 개의 다른 고대 미술품과 건축물은 오늘날에도 계속해서 사람들을 놀라게 한다. 이 훌륭한 작품들은 수 세기 동안 살아남았는데, 이는 사람들이 그것들을 보전하기 위해 큰 노력을 기울였기 때문이다. 그러나 모두가 최상의 보전 방법에 대해 동의하는 것은 아니다. 일부 사람들은 예술품 '복원'을 옹호하고 다른 사람들은 예술품 '보존'을 선호한다. 그렇다면, 이 두 접근법 간의 차이는 무엇인가?

복원가들은 예술품을 청소하고, 보수하고, 때로는 재건한다. 대부분의 복원가들은 예술 교육을 받으며, 시행착오를 거쳐 작업하는 법을 배운다. 그들의 목적은 예술품을 처음 제작되었을 때처럼 보이게 만들어서, 예술품에 예전의 아름다움을 되찾아주는 것이다. 예를 들어, 복원가들은 그림의 색채를 다시 손보거나 조각상의 부서지거나 닳은 부분을 교체할 수 있다.

반면, 예술품 보존가들은 단순히 고대 예술을 가능한 한 최상의 상태로 유지하는 것에 전념한다. 일반적으로 고도로 훈련된 전문가들인 보존가들은 업무 수행에 과학적인 접근법을 취한다. 그들은 예술품에 가급적 손을 대지 않으며 더 이상의 손상이나 마모를 방지하기 위해 반드시 최적의 환경이 되도록 한다.

그러나 보존과 복원은 공통점도 많다. 가장 중요한 점으로, 보존가와 복원가 둘 다의 주된 목표는 예술품의 본래 특징을 유지하는 것이다. 보존가들은 예술품의 원형을 좋은 상태로 유지함으로써 이를 수행한다. 마찬가지로, 복원가들도 예술품을 원형대로 정확히 표현하는 일에 관심이 있다. 그들이 만약 예술품이 원래 어떤 모습이었는지에 관한 믿을 만한 역사적 증거를 찾지 못한다면, 그것에 어떤 복원 작업도 하지 않을 것이다.

어휘 architecture[ɑ́ːrkitèktʃər] 몝 건축; *건축물   amaze[əméiz] 됨 놀라게 하다   preserve[prizə́ːrv] 됨 보호하다, 보전하다 (preservation 몝 보전)   advocate[ǽdvəkèit] 됨 옹호하다   restoration[rèstəréiʃən] 몝 복원 (restorer 몝 복원 전문가)   conservation[kɑ̀nsərvéiʃən] 몝 보존 (conservator 몝 보존자)   approach[əpróutʃ] 몝 접근법   artwork[ɑ́ːrtwə̀ːrk] 몝 미술품   craft[kræft] 몝 (특수한) 기술, 재능   trial and error 시행착오   aim[eim] 몝 목적   former[fɔ́ːrmər] 혭 이전의   glory[glɔ́ːri] 몝 영광; *장관, 아름다움   worn[wɔːrn] 혭 닳은 (wear 몝 닳음, 마모)   be committed to …에 전념하다   condition[kəndíʃən] 몝 상태; (*pl.*) 환경   ensure[inʃúər] 됨 확실히 하다   in common 공통으로   primary[práimeri] 혭 주된   maintain[meintéin] 됨 유지하다 (maintenance 몝 유지, 보수)   likewise[láikwàiz] 뷔 마찬가지로   representation[rèprizentéiʃən] 몝 표현   [문제] controversy[kɑ́ntrəvə̀ːrsi] 몝 논란

optimal[áptəməl] 형 최적의   minimal[mínəməl] 형 최소의

구문 14행 ..., and they learn **how to do** their craft through trial and error.
- how to-v: …하는 방법

15행 Their aim is **to return** artwork to its former glory, [*making* it **look** like …].
- to return: 주격보어로 쓰인 명사적 용법의 to부정사
- making 이하는 동시동작을 나타내는 분사구문
- 사역동사(make) + 목적어 + 동사원형: …가 ~하게 하다

21행 They touch the artwork **as** little **as possible** ….
- as + 부사의 원급 + as possible: 가능한 한 …하게

29행 If they cannot find reliable historical evidence of [**what** the artwork originally looked like], ….
- what 이하는 전치사 of의 목적어 역할을 하는 간접의문문

STRATEGIC ORGANIZER *1)* restoring *2)* repair *3)* changes *4)* maintain *5)* original

EXPANDING KNOWLEDGE

1 d   **2** *1)* T *2)* F

다빈치의 *최후의 만찬*에 대한 가장 최근의 복원은 1999년 5월에 완료되었다. 최우선 과제는 그림의 추가적인 손상을 막는 것이었다. 화학 분석에서 이전 복원에서 채색한 부분이 다빈치 작품의 원본 색을 부식시키고 있다는 점이 드러났다. 복원가들은 최초에 완성된 이후 작품에 더해진 모든 채색을 없애기로 결정했다. 그러한 어려운 작업은 세세한 곳까지 대단한 주의를 필요로 했다. 레이더와 레이저를 비롯한 여러 가지 정교한 기술이 사용되었다. 따라서 복원은 느리고 어려운 과정이었다. 우표 한 장 크기만 한 면적이 여러 단계에 걸쳐 복원될 수 있었다. 결국, 20년간의 힘든 노력이 결실을 맺었다. 그림은 원형의 모습을 온전하게 유지하면서 복원되었다. 오늘날 이 그림은 정교한 공기 여과 장치로 보존되고 있다. 한 번에 25명 이하의 단체들이 15분 동안만 이 그림을 보는 것이 허용된다.

어휘 complete[kəmplíːt] 동 완료하다, 끝마치다   foremost[fɔ́ːrmòust] 형 가장 중요한
deterioration[ditìəriəréiʃən] 명 악화, 훼손   eat away …을 부식시키다
sophisticated[səfístəkèitid] 형 정교한   postage stamp 우표   ultimately[ʌ́ltəmətli] 부 결국,
궁극적으로   pay off 성과를 내다   intact[intǽkt] 형 온전한   filtration[filtréiʃən] 명 여과
[문제] shortage[ʃɔ́ːrtidʒ] 명 부족   uncover[ʌnkʌ́vər] 동 벗겨내다

구문 6행 Restorers decided to remove all the paint [**that** *had been added* to the piece after it was originally finished].
- that 이하는 all the paint를 수식하는 주격 관계대명사절
- had been added: 주절의 시제보다 앞선 시점의 내용을 가리키는 과거완료 수동태

VOCABULARY REVIEW

A **1** advocate **2** intact **3** primary **4** preserve
B **1** artistic **2** deterioration **3** rebuilt **4** pay off **5** restoration **6** sophisticated
C **1** d **2** c

★unit★
13 LIFE SCIENCE pp. 56-59

★Supertaster

1 b **2** c **3** b **4** Because a high salt content disguises bitterness. **5** c **6** c

당신은 브로콜리나 양배추, 커피, 심지어 다크 초콜릿의 맛을 싫어하는가? 그렇다면 당신은 미각이 아주 강한 사람인 '초미각자'일지도 모른다. 초미각자는 특히 쓴맛에 민감한데, 이는 그들이 흔히 양배추나 커피를 싫어하는 이유이다.

미각에 관련해서는, 세 가지 주요 집단의 사람들이 있다. 인구의 약 50퍼센트가 여러 종류의 맛에 대해 보통 범위의 민감성을 가지고 있는 중간 미각자이다. 25퍼센트는 미각이 둔한 미맹이다. 그리고 나머지 25퍼센트의 사람들이 초미각자이다. 초미각자는 다른 사람들보다 미뢰가 더 많고, 그들의 미뢰는 많은 음식에 함유된 특정 화학물질의 쓴맛에 더욱 민감하다. 증거에 따르면 높은 비율의 아프리카와 아시아, 남미인들이 초미각자이며, 여성이 남성보다 초미각자일 가능성이 더 크다.

왜 어떤 사람들은 초미각자일까? 한 이론에 따르면 이 유전자는 유독한 물질로부터 사람을 안전하게 지키도록 진화했다고 한다. 초미각자는 맛으로 위험한 식물을 더 잘 구별해낼 수 있다. 그러나 초미각자가 되는 것은 진화상의 단점도 될 수 있는데, 이는 그들이 중간 미각자나 미맹보다 더 제한된 식사를 하기 때문이다. 또한, 초미각자는 지나치게 기름지거나 단 음식을 싫어하기 때문에 더 건강할지도 모른다고 생각되었다. 그러나 새로운 연구에 의하면 대부분의 초미각자는 매우 짠 음식을 즐기는데, 이는 높은 소금함량이 쓴맛을 가려주기 때문이다.

그렇다면 대체로 보아 초미각자인 것은 이점이자 약점이기도 하다. 초미각자는 비만을 덜 겪지만 그들의 짠 식단은 건강에 부정적인 영향을 미친다. 이것을 극복하기 위해, 그들은 요리를 할 때 더 많은 창의력이 필요하고 음식 선택에 있어서 강한 의지력이 필요하다.

어휘 cabbage[kæbidʒ] 명 양배추 sensitive[sénsətiv] 형 예민한 (sensitivity 명 민감성)
bitterness[bítərnis] 명 쓴맛 dislike[disláik] 동 싫어하다 when it comes to …에 관한
한 taste bud (혀의) 미뢰 specific[spisífik] 형 구체적인; *특정한 chemical[kémikəl]
형 화학의 gene[dʒiːn] 명 유전자 evolve[iválv] 동 진화하다 (evolutionary 형 진화상의)
poisonous[pɔ́izənəs] 형 유독한 distinguish[distíŋgwiʃ] 동 구별하다 limited[límitid] 형 제한적인
overly[óuvərli] 부 매우, 몹시 fatty[fǽti] 형 지방이 많은 content[kántent] 명 내용물; *함유량,
함량 disguise[disgáiz] 동 변장하다; *숨기다 all in all 대체로 mixed blessing 유리하기도 하고
불리하기도 한 것 obesity[oubíːsəti] 명 비만 willpower[wílpàuər] 명 의지력
[문제] tongue[tʌŋ] 명 혀 prevalent[prévələnt] 형 일반적인, 널리 퍼져 있는

구문 2행 Then you might be a "supertaster," someone [**whose** sense of taste is very strong].
• whose 이하는 someone을 수식하는 소유격 관계대명사절
4행 Supertasters are particularly sensitive to bitterness, **which** is (the reason) *why* they often dislike cabbage and coffee.
• which: 앞의 절을 선행사로 하는 계속적 용법의 주격 관계대명사(= and that)
• why: 이유를 나타내는 관계부사로, 앞에 선행사 the reason이 생략되어 있음
16행 One theory is [**that** this gene has evolved to *keep* people *safe* from poisonous substances].
• that: 주격보어 역할을 하는 명사절을 이끄는 접속사
• keep + 목적어 + 형용사: …을 ～한 상태로 유지하다

STRATEGIC SUMMARY sensitive, bitter, majority, poisonous, salty

23

EXPANDING KNOWLEDGE

1 c **2** c

> 당신은 자신이 초미각자인지 궁금한가? 여기 당신이 어떤 종류의 미각자인지 알아볼 수 있는 간단한 검사가 있다. 이 검사는 당신이 가지고 있는 미뢰의 수를 세도록 해준다. 이를 위해서, 당신은 약간의 파란색 식용 색소와 지름 7mm의 구멍이 있는 종이 1장, 그리고 돋보기가 필요할 것이다. 파란색 식용 색소를 혀끝에 묻혀라. 혀가 파란색으로 바뀌겠지만 미뢰가 있는 부분은 그대로 분홍색일 것이다. 종이를 혀에 놓고 돋보기를 사용하여 구멍 안에 있는 분홍색 점의 수를 세라. 개수가 15개보다 적으면, 당신은 미맹이다. 15개와 35개 사이이면, 당신은 중간 미각자이다. 35개가 넘으면 당신은 초미각자이다!

어휘 count[kaunt] ⑧ (수를) 세다 food coloring 식용 색소 magnifying glass 돋보기 tip[tip] ⑲ 끝 dot[dat] ⑲ 점 [문제] appease[əpíːz] ⑧ 달래다; *(식욕 · 호기심 등을) 충족시키다

구문
1행 Do you wonder [**if** you are a supertaster]?
- if: '…인지 (아닌지)'의 의미로, 동사 wonder의 목적어인 명사절을 이끄는 접속사

1행 Here is an easy test [(which[that]) **you** can do] *to find out* [**what** kind of taster you are].
- you 앞에 an easy test를 선행사로 하는 목적격 관계대명사가 생략되어 있음
- to find out: '…하기 위해'라는 의미로, 목적을 나타내는 부사적 용법의 to부정사구
- what 이하는 동사구 find out의 목적어 역할을 하는 간접의문문

5행 …, but the area [**where** your taste buds are] will stay pink.
- where 이하는 the area를 수식하는 관계부사절

VOCABULARY REVIEW

A **1** poisonous **2** willpower **3** distinguish **4** disguise
B **1** blessing **2** fatty **3** tongue **4** sensitive **5** chemical **6** highly
C **1** c **2** b

unit 14 PEOPLE

pp. 60-63

Great Inventors

1 c **2** c **3** a, c **4** d **5** Because he lacked the business sense needed to market his inventions as commercial products. **6** d

> 근대 초기의 가장 위대한 지성인 중 두 명은 니콜라 테슬라와 토머스 에디슨이었다. 하지만 오늘날 학생들은 오직 에디슨의 위대한 업적에 대해서만 배운다. 그들은 테슬라에 대해서는 거의 배우지 않는다. 그런데 어떻게 그의 과학적 공헌이 에디슨의 공헌에 비견한다고 여겨질 수 있을까?
>
> 테슬라는 유능한 과학자이자 발명가였다. 1884년에 세르비아에서 미국으로 온 직후, 그는 다수의 중요한 프로젝트에서 에디슨과 함께 작업하기 시작했다. 에디슨은 갓 전구를 발명하여 전기를 공급할 장치가 필요했다. 그래서 그는 직류(DC) 전기 장치를 만들었고, 그것을 안전하고 효과적인 전기 기술이라고 광고했다. 하지만 테슬라는 DC에 심각한 결함이 있다고 생각했고 그 장치는 전기를 발생시켜 광역 배전망을 통해 전달할 수 없을 것이라는 사실을 알았다. 그런 까닭에, 그는 DC 장치와 직접적인 경쟁 상대가 되는 교류(AC) 장치를 개발했다. 이에 따라, 테슬라는 에디슨을 떠났고 두 위대한 과학자는 평생의 경쟁자가 되었다.

결국, 테슬라의 AC 장치가 이겼고, 오늘날 그것은 수많은 가정에서 사용되고 있다. 에디슨의 전구는 뛰어난 발명품이었지만, 전기를 전달할 실용적이고 믿을 만한 방법이 없었더라면 가치가 거의 없었을 것이다. 테슬라의 AC 장치 덕분에, 에디슨의 전구는 현대 생활의 필수적인 부분이 되었다. 이러한 사실에도 불구하고, 테슬라는 거의 알려지지 않았다.

그 이유를 이해하려면, 우리는 에디슨의 사업 수완을 생각해보아야 한다. 에디슨은 자신의 제품과 자기 자신을 납득시킬 수 있는 뛰어난 자기 홍보가였다. 반면에, 테슬라는 자신의 발명품을 상업적 제품으로 홍보하는 데 필요한 사업 감각이 부족했다. 하지만 비록 니콜라 테슬라의 업적을 기억하는 사람이 거의 없을지라도, 과학에 대한 그의 기여는 에디슨 못지않게 중요하다.

어휘　mind[maind] 몡 마음; *지성(인)　accomplishment[əkámpliʃmənt] 몡 업적, 공적　rarely[réərli] 븠 좀처럼 …하지 않는　contribution[kɑ̀ntrəbjúːʃən] 몡 기여, 공헌　comparable[kámpərəbl] 형 (…와) 필적하는, 비교할 만한　inventor[invéntər] 몡 발명가 (invent 동 발명하다　invention 몡 발명품)　electric light bulb 전구　distribute[distríbjuːt] 동 분배하다; *공급하다　direct current 직류　market[máːrkit] 동 (상품을) 내놓다[광고하다]　drawback[drɔ́ːbæ̀k] 몡 결점, 문제점　generate[dʒénərèit] 동 발생시키다, 만들어내다　grid[grid] 몡 격자 무늬; *배전망　alternating current 교류　competitor[kəmpétətər] 몡 경쟁자, 경쟁 상대　lifelong[láiflɔ̀ːŋ] 형 평생 동안의, 일생의　win out 수행해내다; *이기다　brilliant[bríljənt] 형 훌륭한; *뛰어난, 우수한　practical[præktikəl] 형 실용적인　virtually[vɔ́ːrtʃuəli] 븠 사실상, 거의　sell[sel] 동 팔다; *납득시키다　commercial[kəmɔ́ːrʃəl] 형 상업적인　[문제] multi-talented[mʌ̀ltitǽləntid] 형 다재다능한　defective[diféktiv] 형 결함이 있는

구문　3행　Rarely **are they** taught about Tesla.
　　• are they: 부정어(rarely)가 문장 앞에 와서 주어와 동사가 도치됨
　　7행　Edison **had** just **invented** the electric light bulb and needed a system *to distribute* electricity.
　　• had invented: 과거 기준 시점까지의 동작의 완료를 나타내는 과거완료
　　• to distribute: a system을 수식하는 형용사적 용법의 to부정사
　　8행　…, he created the direct current (DC) electricity system, **which** he marketed ….
　　• which: the direct current (DC) electricity system을 보충 설명하는 계속적 용법의 목적격 관계대명사
　　16행　… it **would have been** of little value **without** a practical and reliable way ….
　　• '…가 없었다면, ~했을 텐데'의 의미의 가정법 과거완료 문장으로, without이 이끄는 구가 if절을 대신함
　　23행　Tesla, on the other hand, lacked the business sense [**needed** to market …].
　　• needed 이하는 the business sense를 수식하는 과거분사구
　　26행　…, his contributions to science are just **as important as** *those* of Edison, ….
　　• as + 형용사의 원급 + as: …만큼 ~한
　　• those: contributions to science를 대신하는 대명사

STRATEGIC SUMMARY　forgotten, invented, deliver, inefficient, promote

EXPANDING KNOWLEDGE

1 c　**2** b

19세기 후반, 전류 전쟁이 벌어지고 있었다. 한쪽에는 DC 장치를 가진 토머스 에디슨이 있었다. 다른 한쪽에는 AC 장치를 가진 조지 웨스팅하우스와 니콜라 테슬라가 있었다. 전환점은 나이아가라 폭포에서 발생했다. 조지 웨스팅하우스는 테슬라의 AC 장치를 이용하여 폭포에서 전기를 생산하는 계약을 따냈다. 하지만 많은 사람들이

AC 장치가 뉴욕 버펄로 인근 도시에 충분한 전력을 발생시킬 수 있을지에 의문을 가졌다. 반면에 테슬라는 그 장치가 버펄로뿐만 아니라, 동부 해안 지방 전역에도 충분한 전력을 발생시킬 수 있을 것이라 확신했다. 1896년 11월 16일, 마침내 테슬라는 나이아가라 폭포에서 전기를 일으켜 버펄로에 보냄으로써, 회의적인 사람들이 틀렸다는 것을 증명했다. 테슬라의 AC 발전기가 효과가 있었던 것이다! 나이아가라 폭포는 테슬라의 AC 장치의 <u>우월성</u>을 증명해주었고, 20세기 초반에 이르러 직류는 대규모 발전의 역사에서 그저 하나의 추억거리가 되었다.

어휘   turning point 전환점   contract[kántrækt] 명 계약   power[páuər] 명 힘; *전기
   nearby[nìərbái] 형 인근의   entire[intáiər] 형 전체의, 온   seaboard[sí:bɔ̀:rd] 명 해안 지방
   skeptic[sképtik] 명 회의론자, 의심이 많은 사람   generator[dʒénərèitər] 명 발전기   work[wə:rk]
   동 일하다; *효과가 있다   mass[mæs] 형 대량의, 대규모의   [문제] superiority[səpìərió:rəti]
   명 우월, 우수   acceptance[ækséptəns] 명 수용

구문   2행   On **one** side *was Thomas Edison* with his DC system. On **the other** (side) *were George Westinghouse and Nikola Tesla* with their AC system.
     • one ... the other ~: (2개 중) 하나는 … 다른 하나는 ~
     • 장소를 나타내는 부사구가 문장 앞에 와서 주어와 동사가 도치됨
  9행   ... the system could generate enough power for **not only** Buffalo, **but also** the entire eastern seaboard.
     • not only A but also B: A뿐만 아니라 B도

VOCABULARY REVIEW

A   **1** brilliant   **2** lack   **3** skeptic   **4** contract
B   **1** generate   **2** in the end   **3** lifelong   **4** turning point   **5** skilled   **6** market
C   **1** d   **2** b

unit
15 JOBS

pp. 64-67

An Interview with a Criminal Profiler

1 a   **2** *1)* b *2)* c *3)* a   **3** narrow down the possible suspects in a case, predict what the criminal might do next   **4** b   **5** b   **6** d

범죄 심리 분석관은 범죄를 수사하는 사람들이며, 요즘 영화와 TV 드라마에서 매우 인기를 얻고 있다. 다음은 한 범죄 심리 분석관과의 인터뷰이다.

Q: 범죄 심리 분석이란 무엇입니까?
A: 범죄 심리 분석은 기본적으로 범죄자의 마음속에 들어가려고 애쓰는 것입니다. 증거를 바탕으로, 우리는 그들이 어떻게 생각하고 어떤 종류의 사람인지 알아내려고 노력합니다. 이것은 경찰들이 한 사건에서 유력한 용의자들을 좁혀나갈 수 있게 합니다. 그것은 또한 경찰들로 하여금 범죄자들이 다음번에 무엇을 할지 예측할 수 있게 도와줍니다.
Q: 범죄 심리 분석이 중요한 역할을 한 사건들이 있었습니까?
A: 물론이죠. James A. Brussel은 '미치광이 폭파범' 사건에서 형사들을 도운 것으로 유명합니다. 1940년에서 1956년 사이에, 한 연쇄 폭파범이 뉴욕을 공포에 떨게 하고 있었습니다. 범죄 현장과 '미치광이 폭파범'이 남긴 편지에서 나온 증거를 이용하여, Brussel은 그 범죄자의 인물 개요를 구축했습니다. 그는 경찰에게 과체중이며 독신이고, 천주교 신자이면서 예전에 한 에너지 회사에서 일했던 코네티컷 출신의 남성 정비공을 찾으라고 말해주었습니다.

아니나 다를까, 몇 주 후 경찰은 미치광이 폭파범인 George Metersky를 찾아냈고, 그는 이러한 모든 특징에 들어맞았습니다. 심지어 그가 입고 있던 옷까지도 Brussel의 예측과 일치했습니다!

Q: 당신의 직업이 TV에서 근사하게 묘사되고 있다고 생각하십니까?

A: 네, 그렇습니다. *크리미널 마인드*와 같은 프로그램은 우리가 순전히 우리 힘만으로 범죄자들을 찾아내고 잡는 일을 책임지는 것처럼 보이게 합니다. 하지만 현실에서 심리 분석에는 <u>한계</u>가 있습니다. 우리는 보통 범죄자들을 찾아낼 수 없습니다. 우리가 할 수 있는 전부는 범죄자인 사람의 유형을 밝혀내는 것이며, 그 특정 성격 유형에 부합하는 용의자는 10명 혹은 그 이상일지도 모릅니다. 그러니 우리의 역할은 사실상 일반적인 수사 업무를 하는 경찰들을 돕는 것입니다.

어휘	
	criminal[krímənl] ⑲ 범죄의 ⑲ 범죄자 profiler[próufailər] ⑲ 프로필 작가; *범죄 심리 분석관 (profile ⑲ 개요 profiling ⑲ 자료[정보]수집) investigate[invéstəgèit] ⑤ 조사하다, 수사하다 work out 해결하다, 답을 알아내다 narrow down 좁히다, 줄이다 suspect[sʌ́spekt] ⑲ 용의자 predict[pridíkt] ⑤ 예측하다 (prediction ⑲ 예측, 예상) detective[ditéktiv] ⑲ 형사, 수사관 ⑲ 수사의 bomber[bámər] ⑲ 폭파범 serial[síəriəl] ⑲ 상습적인, 연쇄적인 terrorize[térəràiz] ⑤ 공포에 떨게 하다 overweight[óuvərwèit] ⑲ 과체중의, 비만의 Roman Catholic 천주교의 mechanic[məkǽnik] ⑲ 정비공 sure enough 아니나 다를까 fit[fit] ⑤ 들어맞다 identify[aidéntəfài] ⑤ 확인하다; *찾다, 발견하다 [문제] cooperation[kouàpəréiʃən] ⑲ 협력, 협동 romanticize[roumǽntəsàiz] ⑤ 근사하게 묘사하다 priority[praió:rəti] ⑲ 우선권 limitation[lìmətéiʃən] ⑲ 제한, 한계 prohibition[pròuibíʃən] ⑲ 금지

구문		
	6행	..., we try to work out [**how** they think] and [**what** sort of person they are]. • how와 what 이하는 동사구 work out의 목적어 역할을 하는 간접의문문
	14행	... crime scenes and from letters [**left** behind by the "Mad Bomber,"] .... • left 이하는 letters를 수식하는 과거분사구
	16행	..., Roman Catholic, male mechanic from Connecticut [**who** *used to work* for an energy company]. • who 이하는 male mechanic을 수식하는 주격 관계대명사절 • used to-v: (과거에) …하곤 했다
	19행	Even the clothes [(which[that]) **he wore**] matched Brussel's prediction! • he wore 앞에 the clothes를 선행사로 하는 목적격 관계대명사가 생략되어 있음
	22행	Shows like *Criminal Minds* **make** it **seem** *like* we are responsible for identifying and catching criminals all **by ourselves**. • 사역동사(make) + 목적어 + 동사원형: …가 ~하게 하다 • like: '마치 …처럼'의 의미의 접속사 • by oneself: 혼자서

STRATEGIC ORGANIZER   mind, predicts, clues, specific, type

EXPANDING KNOWLEDGE

1 a   **2** *1)* F *2)* T

지문, DNA, 그리고 혈액으로 당신은 무엇을 할 수 있는가? 그야 물론 범죄를 해결한다! 범죄를 해결하기 위해 과학을 <u>이용하는 것은 범죄 과학이라고 불린다.</u> 범죄 과학자들은 경찰이 용의자와 범죄 현장을 연결하도록 돕는다. 그들의 임무는 인체를 연구하는 것부터 날씨 패턴을 추적하는 것까지 모든 것을 포함한다. 때때로 그들은 정확한 사인을 밝히기 위해 시체를 상세히 검안하기도 한다. 다른 때에는, 약물이나 폭발물의 흔적을 찾는다. 그들은 심지어 사망할 당시 사람의 나이를 밝혀내기 위해 뼈를 살펴볼 수도 있다. 그들은 살인자를 찾아내기 위해 물어뜯은 연필에 남아 있는 침이나 피부 조각에서 나온 DNA를 이용할 수도 있다. 범죄 과학자들의 노력 덕분에, 범죄 해결이 훨씬 더 쉬워졌다.

fingerprint[fíŋgərprìnt] 명 지문　why[hwai] 갑 어머, 그야　forensics[fərénsiks] 명 범죄 과학
(forensic 형 법의학의, 범죄 과학 수사의)　track[træk] 동 추적하다　carry out 수행하다, 이행하다
detailed[ditéild] 형 상세한　examination[igzæmənéiʃən] 명 검사　determine[ditə́ːrmin]
동 알아내다, 밝히다　explosive[iksplóusiv] 명 폭발물　saliva[səláivə] 명 침　chew[tʃuː] 동 씹다;
*물어뜯다　flake[fleik] 명 조각　murderer[mə́ːrdərər] 명 살인자
[문제] inspect[inspékt] 동 검사하다

구문　2행　Forensic scientists help police **link** suspects **to** crime senses.
　　　• link A to B: A와 B를 연결하다
　　9행　Thanks to the work of forensic scientists, solving crimes has become **much** easier.
　　　• much: '훨씬'의 의미로, 비교급을 강조하는 부사

VOCABULARY REVIEW

A　**1** predict　**2** investigate　**3** fit　**4** romanticize
B　**1** narrow down　**2** by myself　**3** criminal　**4** evidence　**5** limitations　**6** work out
C　**1** d　**2** c

16 BIOLOGY

pp. 68-71

*Dreams

1 c　**2** c　**3** c　**4** c　**5** Because while we dream, the part of the brain responsible for logical thinking shuts off, and the emotional part of the brain takes over.　**6** 1) F　2) F

뇌는 놀라운 기관이다. 매일 밤, 뇌는 진짜처럼 보이는 장소와 상황에 대한 생생한 이미지를 만들어낼 수 있다. 이것이 꿈의 세계이다. 수 세기 동안, 사람들은 꿈에 관한 여러 이론을 접했다. 지난 몇십 년에 걸친 뇌 스캔 기술의 발달로, 우리는 이제 꿈에 관한 몇 가지 사실을 이해할 수 있다.

잠자는 동안 뇌의 일부는 아주 활발해진다. 뇌에서 아주 많은 활동이 일어나고 있으므로, 꿈을 기억하는 일이 쉬울 것처럼 보인다. 그러나 실제로 사람들은 자신들의 꿈의 5퍼센트도 기억하지 못한다. 이것은 수면 중 뇌의 일부가 활동을 재개하는 반면 다른 부분은 그렇지 않고, 그것이 뇌의 화학적 성질에 변화를 주기 때문이다. 이 화학적인 변화 때문에 꿈의 내용은 단기 기억에 저장되고 장기 기억으로 이전될 수 없다. (장기 기억을 향상할 수 있는 몇 가지 방법이 있다.) 따라서 당신이 깨어나자마자 기록하지 않으면 꿈을 기억하는 것이 불가능하다.

꿈에 관한 또 다른 특징은 꿈이 얼마나 <u>무작위적이고 비논리적일</u> 수 있는가이다. 꿈을 꾸는 동안 뇌에서 논리적 사고를 관장하는 부분이 멈추고, 감정을 담당하는 부분이 더 활성화된다. 이것이 흔히 우리의 꿈이 매우 감정적이면서도 특이한 내용으로 가득 차 있는 이유이다. 예를 들어, 당신은 슈퍼맨처럼 하늘 위로 높이 날거나 좋아하는 만화 등장인물과 함께 신나는 모험을 하는 꿈을 꿀지도 모른다. 꿈의 세계에서는 우리가 상상할 수 있는 것은 무엇이든 가능해진다.

최근의 기술 진보로 과학자들은 꿈이 어떻게 만들어지는지 더 잘 이해하게 되었다. 그럼에도 불구하고 꿈과 뇌 사이의 관계를 완전히 이해하기 위해서는 더 많은 연구가 필요하다.

어휘　organ[ɔ́ːrgən] 명 (인체 내의) 기관　vivid[vívid] 형 생생한　reactivate[riǽktəvèit] 동 (활동 등을) 재개하다　chemistry[kéməstri] 명 화학; *화학적 성질 (chemical 형 화학적인)　content[kántent] 명 내용　short-term[ʃɔ́ːrttə̀ːrm] 형 단기의　transfer[trænsfə́ːr] 동 옮기다, 이전하다　long-term[lɔ́ːŋtə̀ːrm] 형 장기의　shut off (기계 · 기구 등이) 멈추다[서다]　take over 더 커지다[중요해지다]

unusual[ʌnjúːʒuəl] 혱 특이한, 흔치 않은   advance[ædvǽns] 뗑 진보   nevertheless[nèvərðəlés]
빗 그럼에도 불구하고   fully[fúli] 빗 완전히, 충분히   [문제] interpret[intə́ːrprit] 똉 해석하다
additional[ədíʃənl] 혱 추가의   odd[ad] 혱 이상한   random[rǽndəm] 혱 무작위의
illogical[ilάdʒikəl] 혱 비논리적인

구문   1행   … create vivid images of places and situations [**that** *seem real*].
· that 이하는 vivid images of places and situations를 수식하는 주격 관계대명사절
· seem + 형용사: …인 것 같다, …처럼 보이다

6행   **With** so much activity **going on** in the brain, it seems that ….
· with + 명사 + v-ing: '…가 ~한 채로'라는 의미의 분사구문으로, 명사와 분사가 능동 관계일 때 현재분사를 씀

9행   … some parts of the brain are reactivated during sleep while others **are not** (reactivated), [*changing* the brain's chemistry].
· are not 뒤에 반복되는 부분인 reactivated가 생략됨
· changing 이하는 연속동작을 나타내는 분사구문

13행   …, **it** is not possible [**to remember** your dreams] *unless* you record them ….
· it은 가주어이고, to remember 이하가 진주어
· unless: …하지 않는 한(= if … not)

16행   …, the part of the brain [(which[that] is) **responsible** for logical thinking] shuts off, ….
· responsible 앞에 '주격 관계대명사 + be동사'가 생략되어 있음

23행   In the world of dreams, anything [(that) **we** can imagine] becomes possible.
· we 앞에 anything을 선행사로 하는 목적격 관계대명사가 생략되어 있음

STRATEGIC SUMMARY   active, chemical, long-term, illogical, logical

EXPANDING KNOWLEDGE

1 c   **2** b

동물들이 꿈을 꿀까? 자고 있는 동물들은 눈꺼풀을 실룩거리고 다리와 발을 움직이면서 꿈을 꾸는 것처럼 행동한다. 동물들이 정말로 꿈을 꾼다면, 어떤 종류의 꿈을 꾸고 그 목적은 무엇일까?

과학자들은 쥐가 어떤 꿈을 꾸는지 알아내기 위해 쥐를 연구했다. 그 연구에서 연구원들은 미로 속을 뛰어다니는 쥐의 뇌 활동을 관찰했다. 그들은 쥐가 미로의 각 부분에서 독특한 뇌 활동 패턴을 보인다는 것을 알아냈다. 그런 다음 연구원들은 그 동물들이 자고 있는 동안의 그들의 뇌 활동을 조사했다. 그들은 쥐의 절반 정도가 미로를 돌아다닐 때와 같은 뇌 활동 패턴을 보인다는 것을 발견했다. 이는 쥐들이 꿈에서 미로 속을 달리는 연습을 하고, 이로써 실제의 미로를 통과하기 위한 준비가 더 많이 될 수 있게 한다는 것을 시사한다.

이 연구는 대부분의 동물이 꿈을 꿀 수 있을 뿐만 아니라 이전에 생각되던 것보다 더 복잡한 꿈도 꾼다는 것을 시사한다.

어휘   twitch[twitʃ] 똉 실룩거리다   eyelid[áilìd] 뗑 눈꺼풀   paw[pɔː] 뗑 (동물의) 발
monitor[mάnətər] 똉 감시하다; *관찰하다   maze[meiz] 뗑 미로   portion[pɔ́ːrʃən] 뗑 부분
complete[kəmplíːt] 똉 완수하다   be capable of …을 할 수 있다   complex[kάmpleks] 혱 복잡한
previously[príːviəsli] 빗 이전에

구문   2행   If they **do** dream, what kinds of dreams do they have …?
· do: 동사 dream을 강조하는 조동사

10행   … doing so **enabled** them **to be** more prepared to complete the actual maze.
· enable + 목적어 + to-v: …가 ~할 수 있게 하다

VOCABULARY REVIEW

A **1** portion **2** reactivate **3** random **4** transfer
B **1** in reality **2** complete **3** twitched **4** capable of **5** eyelids **6** long-term
C **1** c **2** d

unit 17 MEDICINE

pp. 72-75

Placebo Effect

1 a **2** c **3** c **4** d **5** encouraging patients' brains to get rid of pain naturally **6** *1)* T *2)* F

아플 때 약을 먹으면 보통 몸이 나아진다. 그런데 어떤 경우에는 약을 먹고 있다고 생각하는 것만으로도 통증을 없애기에 충분하다. 플라세보로 알려진 이런 종류의 가짜 치료법은 의사와 연구원에 의해 오랫동안 사용되었다. 놀랍게도 '플라세보 효과'는 종종 환자들이 상태가 나아지고 건강이 향상되게 해준다.

플라세보는 설탕으로 만든 알약이나 가짜 크림 그리고 기타 성분을 비롯한 여러 가지 형태로 나올 수 있다. 그것들은 연구원들이 약품을 시험하는 실험에서 흔히 사용된다. 연구원들은 일부 환자들에게는 플라세보를 주고 다른 환자들에게는 진짜 약을 준다. 이는 그들로 하여금 약이 얼마나 효과가 있는지 판정할 수 있게 해준다. 그런데 설탕으로 만든 알약을 먹는 것이 어떻게 몸 상태를 나아지게 할 수 있을까?

약을 먹으면 뇌는 무언가 긍정적인 일이 생길 것이라 예상한다. 통증 완화와 같은 보상을 받을 수 있다는 기대감이 뇌에서 기분을 좋게 만드는 특수 화학물질인 도파민을 방출하도록 한다. 플라세보와 같은 가짜 약을 복용할 때도 같은 뇌의 작용이 일어난다. 통증이 사라질 것이라 생각하는 것만으로 뇌를 자극하여 이런 자연 진통제를 방출하게 하고 실제로 통증을 없애는 데 도움이 된다.

물론, 플라세보는 실제 의학적 치료를 대체하는 역할은 하지 못한다. 그러나 플라세보 효과가 어떻게 작용하는지를 이해함으로써 과학자들은 통증을 겪는 환자들을 도울 새로운 방법을 찾을 수 있을지도 모른다. 아마 미래에 의사들은 환자를 낫게 하려고 위험 소지가 있는 약을 처방하는 대신, 환자들의 뇌가 자연스럽게 통증을 없애도록 촉진할 방법을 찾아낼 것이다.

어휘 take medicine 약을 먹다 go away 사라지다 fake[feik] 혱 가짜의 pill[pil] 몡 알약
substance[sʌ́bstəns] 몡 물질 expect[ikspékt] 통 기대하다 (expectation 몡 예상, 기대)
reward[riwɔ́ːrd] 몡 보상 relief[rilíːf] 몡 안도, 안심; *(고통 등의) 완화 release[rilíːs] 통 방출하다
몡 방출 dopamine[dóupəmìːn] 몡 도파민 prompt[prɑmpt] 통 자극하다 painkiller[péinkìlər]
몡 진통제 get rid of …을 없애다 replacement[ripléismənt] 몡 대체; *대체물
potentially[pəténʃəli] 閉 잠재적으로 encourage[inkə́ːridʒ] 통 격려하다; *촉진하다, 조장하다
[문제] analyze[ǽnəlàiz] 통 분석하다 anticipation[æntìsəpéiʃən] 몡 예상, 기대 trigger[trígər]
통 촉발하다 ingredient[ingríːdiənt] 몡 재료, 성분

구문 3행 … thinking that we are taking medicine is **enough to *make*** the pain *go* away.
• enough to-v: …하기에 충분한
• 사역동사(make) + 목적어 + 동사원형: …가 ～하게 하다

7행 …, the "placebo effect" often **leaves** patients **feeling** better and **experiencing** improved health.
• leave + 목적어 + v-ing: …을 ～한 상태가 되게 하다

15행 When you take medicine, your brain **expects** *something positive* **to happen**.
• expect + 목적어 + to-v: …가 ～하기를 기대하다
• something positive: -thing으로 끝나는 대명사는 형용사가 뒤에서 수식함

19행 Just thinking that your pain is going to go away **prompts** the brain **to release** these natural painkillers ....
  • prompt + 목적어 + to-v: ⋯가 ~하도록 자극하다[촉구하다]

STRATEGIC SUMMARY relieve, enough, same, natural, replace

EXPANDING KNOWLEDGE

1 a **2** b

최근에 한 과학자팀이 뇌가 비만에 어떤 역할을 하는지 알아내기 위해 한 무리의 쥐에게 대량의 정크푸드를 먹였다.

과학자인 Paul Johnson과 그의 팀은 쥐들이 정크푸드를 먹으면 먹을수록 전반적으로 더 많이 먹기를 원한다는 것을 발견했다. 이런 행동은 약물 중독과 아주 흡사하며 비만과 약물 중독의 뇌 화학작용이 비슷할 수도 있음을 시사한다. 이를 증명하기 위해 과학자들은 쥐 뇌의 쾌락 중추를 연구했다. 그들은 정크푸드를 먹은 쥐는 만족감을 느끼려면 평범한 식단을 섭취한 쥐보다 훨씬 더 많이 먹어야 한다는 것을 발견했다. 이런 자제력의 상실은 중독의 명백한 징후이다. 궁극적으로 정크푸드를 먹은 쥐는 건강에 해로운 식단을 포기하기를 거부했다.

이 연구는 과학자들이 어떻게 뇌 안의 화학물질이 사람들을 과식하고 살찌게 하는지 이해하는 데 도움을 주었다.

어휘 feed[fi:d] ⑧ 먹이를 주다 addiction[ədíkʃən] ⑲ 중독 consume[kənsú:m] ⑧ 소모하다; *먹다, 마시다 ultimately[ʌ́ltəmətli] ⑨ 궁극적으로, 결국 overeat[òuvərí:t] ⑧ 과식하다 gain weight 살이 찌다 [문제] appetite[ǽpətàit] ⑲ 식욕 promote[prəmóut] ⑧ 촉진하다 digestion[didʒéstʃən] ⑲ 소화

구문 4행 ... **the more** junk food the rats ate, **the more** the animals wanted to eat in general.
  • the + 비교급 ..., the + 비교급 ~: ⋯하면 할수록 더 ~하다
9행 ... the rats [**that** ate junk food] needed to eat *much* more in order to feel pleasure than the rats [**that** consumed a normal diet].
  • that 이하는 각각 앞의 the rats를 수식하는 주격 관계대명사절
  • much: '훨씬'의 의미로, 비교급을 강조하는 부사
12행 ... how chemicals in the brain **cause** people **to overeat** and (to) **gain** weight.
  • cause + 목적어 + to-v: ⋯가 ~하게 하다

VOCABULARY REVIEW

A **1** loss **2** relief **3** painkiller **4** replacement
B **1** overeat **2** expectation **3** reward **4** addiction **5** prompted **6** get rid of
C **1** d **2** b

unit
18 HEALTH
pp. 76-79

*Carbohydrate Addiction

1 d **2** d **3** c **4** a **5** Because they are rich in vitamins, minerals, fibers, and other healthy substances. **6** *1)* F *2)* T

Jay 박사님께,

저는 건강한 식사를 하려고 최선을 다합니다. 하지만 때때로 밤늦거나 심지어 식사 직후에도 빵이나 파스타가 몹시 먹고 싶어집니다. 왜 이러한 욕구를 느끼는 것이고, 이를 피하려면 어떻게 해야 하나요?

Bella

Bella에게,

저는 무엇이 문제인지 알 것 같습니다. 당신은 탄수화물 중독이군요. 케이크에서부터 스파게티와 브로콜리에 이르는 모든 것에 탄수화물이 있습니다. 이러한 음식을 먹으면, 인체는 인슐린을 이용하여 탄수화물을 더 단순한 형태의 당분으로 분해하고, 이것이 에너지를 공급해줍니다. 그것에는 잘못된 것이 없습니다. 하지만 너무 많은 양의 탄수화물 섭취는 체내의 인슐린 수치를 높여 탄수화물 당분을 지나치게 빨리 소비하게 합니다. 이는 당신의 몸이 당신이 사용하고 있는 당분을 모두 대체할 필요가 있다고 느끼기 때문에 결과적으로 허기지게 합니다. 당신은 이제 점점 더 많은 탄수화물을 먹는 중독 사이클에 갇힌 것입니다. 다른 중독처럼, 이러한 습관은 건강에 좋지 않습니다. 그 모든 탄수화물 당은 비만, 당뇨, 심장병과 같은 심각한 질병으로 이어질 수 있습니다.

하지만 탄수화물을 함유한 음식을 섭취하는 것은 여전히 중요합니다. 최근에, 소위 '무(無) 탄수화물' 식이요법이 매우 인기를 얻었습니다. 하지만 사실 이러한 식단은 탄수화물 중독만큼이나 건강에 해로울 수 있습니다. 탄수화물은 유해한 것이 아닙니다. 전문가들은 탄수화물이 식단에서 열량의 절반 정도를 차지해야 한다고 말합니다. 탄수화물을 함유한 대부분의 과일과 채소에는 비타민, 무기질, 섬유질과 그 밖의 건강에 좋은 물질들도 풍부합니다. 그러므로 탄수화물을 함유하고 있다고 해서 식단에서 과일과 채소를 제외하는 것은 건강에 좋은 많은 것들도 제외한다는 것을 의미합니다. 가장 좋은 것은 탄수화물을 적절히 섭취하고 그중 일부를 반드시 과일, 채소, 곡물, 그리고 저지방 유제품과 같이 추가적인 건강한 성분이 들어있는 식품들로부터 얻도록 하는 것입니다.

Jay 박사

어휘 craving[kréiviŋ] 명 열망, 갈망　carbohydrate[kà:rbouháidreit] 명 탄수화물　break down 부수다; *분해하다　diabetes[dàiəbí:tis] 명 당뇨병　expert[ékspə:rt] 명 전문가　make up 이루다, 형성하다　mineral[mínərəl] 명 무기질　fiber[fáibər] 명 섬유질　cut[kʌt] 동 자르다; *없애다, 배제하다　stuff[stʌf] 명 것, 물건　in moderation 적당히　low-fat[lóufǽt] 형 저지방의　dairy[déəri] 명 유제품　element[éləmənt] 명 요소, 성분　[문제] blame[bleim] 동 …을 탓하다　exclude[iksklú:d] 동 제외하다

구문

10행　… to break down the carbohydrates into simpler forms of sugar, **which** provide energy.
　• which: simpler forms of sugar를 보충 설명하는 계속적 용법의 주격 관계대명사(= and they)

13행　But [**eating** a lot of carbohydrates] raises the body's level of insulin, [*causing* you **to consume** the carbohydrate sugar too quickly].
　• eating 이하는 문장의 주어 역할을 하는 동명사구
　• causing 이하는 연속동작을 나타내는 분사구문(= and it causes)
　• cause + 목적어 + to-v: …가 ~하게 하다

24행　So **cutting** fruits and vegetables **out of** your diet [*just because* they have carbohydrates] means you're also cutting out lots of healthy stuff.
　• cut A out of B: A를 B로부터 제외하다
　• just because: 단지 …라고 해서

STRATEGIC ORGANIZER　amount, hunger, source, healthy, moderation

EXPANDING KNOWLEDGE

1 b　**2** c

다이어트 콜라를 마시는데도 여전히 체중이 증가하는 사람들은 자신들의 잘못된 식습관을 탓하면 된다. 예를 들어, 건강한 식사를 하는 사람은 일반 콜라 대신에 다이어트 콜라를 마셔서 체중을 감량할 수 있다. 그러나 고칼로리 식사를 상쇄하기 위해 다이어트 콜라를 마시는 사람은 계속 살이 찌게 될 것이다. 이러한 사람들은 다이어트 콜라를 마시면 그들이 원하는 것은 무엇이든 먹어도 된다고 잘못 생각해서, 결국 일반 콜라를 마시면 그러는 것보다 훨씬 더 많은 칼로리를 섭취하게 된다. 게다가 새로운 증거는 다이어트 콜라를 마시는 것이 식욕을 돋우고 단 음식에 대한 욕구를 증가시켜, 간접적인 체중 증가를 야기한다는 것을 보여준다. 결국, 체중을 감량하고 싶다면, 물을 마시고 건강한 식사를 하는 것이 최선의 해결책이다.

어휘   in place of ··· 대신에   compensate[kámpənsèit] 동 보상하다; *보완하다, 상쇄하다   end up 결국 ···으로 되다   stimulate[stímjulèit] 동 자극하다, 활발하게 하다   indirect[ìndərékt] 형 간접적인   overall[óuvərɔ̀ːl] 부 종합적으로, 결국   [문제] myth[miθ] 명 신화; *근거 없는 믿음   substitute[sʌ́bstətjùːt] 동 대신하다, 대용하다

구문   1행   People [**who** drink diet cola and still gain weight] can blame their poor diets.
　　　　　　• who 이하는 people을 수식하는 주격 관계대명사절
　　　5행   … that drinking diet cola will **allow** them **to eat** whatever they want, ….
　　　　　　• allow + 목적어 + to-v: ···가 ~하게 하다
　　　　　　• whatever: '···하는 것은 무엇이든지'라는 의미의 복합관계대명사(= anything that)

VOCABULARY REVIEW

A   **1** dairy   **2** craving   **3** stimulate   **4** element
B   **1** broken down   **2** in moderation   **3** in place of   **4** compensate for   **5** appetite   **6** obesity
C   **1** c   **2** a

unit
19 TRAVEL
pp. 80-83

Derinkuyu Underground City

1 d   **2** d   **3** b   **4** It can be opened and closed from the inside but not from the outside.   **5** c
6 1) T   2) T

이 유네스코 세계 문화유산을 방문하기 전에, 나는 인터넷으로 약간 조사를 했다. 한 사이트에서는 미로처럼 연결된 방과 어둠과 축축한 공기로 이동을 제한하는 복도를 묘사해 놓았다. 그러한 장소에서 내가 얼마나 오래 머무를 수 있을지 궁금했다. Derinkuyu 지하도시라는 그 이름은 내게 일종의 미래 도시를 상상하게 했다. 하지만 그것은 사실 4세기에 로마 제국으로부터 그리고 7세기에 이슬람의 억압으로부터 은신할 곳으로 기독교인들에 의해 지어졌다.

　　일단 안으로 들어갔을 때, 나는 조심스럽게 가이드를 따라갔는데, 오직 그만이 나가는 길을 알았기 때문이다. 나는 기거나 등을 구부리고 걸어서 침실, 부엌, 창고, 학교와 마구간을 지나갔다. 나는 그 복합 건물의 단 10퍼센트만이 대중들에게 공개되어 있다는 것을 읽은 적이 있었지만, 그것은 끝이 없는 것처럼 보였다. 가이드는 이 10퍼센트가 깊이 85미터로, 여덟 개의 층이 있다고 설명해주었다. 그는 그 전체 복합 건물이 2만 명에서 5만 명까지 수용할 수 있다고 말했다. 나는 좁은 터널 하나가 수 킬로미터나 떨어진 또 다른 지하 도시로 이어진다는 것을 들었을 때 놀라움을 감출 수 없었다. 많은 석유 램프가 타고 있었음에도 불구하고, 나는 무척 편안하게 호흡을 할 수 있어서, 내가 지하 여러 층 밑에 있다는 것을 거의 잊어버렸다.

가장 인상적인 특징은 적의 공격으로부터 지하도시를 방어하기 위해 지어진 거대한 문이었다. 그것은 안에서는 열리고 닫힐 수 있었지만, 밖에서는 그렇지 못했다. 그것이 나로 하여금 이 사람들이 마주했을 고난에 대해서 생각하게 했다. 이 고난이 그들을 태양으로부터 숨게 했지만, 그들의 종교적 신념은 그들이 그것을 극복하고 살아남을 수 있게 해주었다.

어휘 World Heritage Site 세계 문화유산   corridor[kɔ́:ridər] 몡 복도   restrict[ristríkt] 통 제한하다
damp[dæmp] 혱 축축한, 습기 찬   empire[émpaiər] 몡 제국   oppression[əpréʃən] 몡 억압, 탄압
crawl[krɔːl] 통 기다, 기어가다   bent[bent] 혱 등이 굽은, 등을 구부린   storage[stɔ́:ridʒ]
몡 저장   stable[stéibl] 몡 마구간   complex[kámpleks] 몡 복합 건물, (건물) 단지   endless[éndlis]
혱 끝없는   house[hauz] 통 수용하다, 거처를 제공하다   contain[kəntéin] 통 포함하다;
*(감정을) 억누르다[참다]   breathe[briːð] 통 호흡하다   impressive[imprésiv] 혱 인상적인
(impress 통 깊은 인상을 주다)   defend[difénd] 통 방어하다   hardship[há:rdʃip] 몡 어려움,
곤란   conviction[kənvíkʃən] 몡 유죄 선고; *신념   [문제] faith[feiθ] 몡 믿음; *신앙(심)
accommodate[əkámədèit] 통 공간을 제공하다, 수용하다

구문 2행   One website described rooms [**connected** like a maze] and corridors [*that* restrict movement with darkness and damp air].
- connected 이하는 rooms를 수식하는 과거분사구
- that 이하는 corridors를 수식하는 주격 관계대명사절

3행   I wondered [**how** long I could stay in such a place].
- how 이하는 동사 wondered의 목적어 역할을 하는 간접의문문

8행   **Once** (I was) inside, I followed my guide carefully, *as* only he knew the way out.
- once: '일단 …하면, 하자마자'라는 의미의 접속사로, 뒤에 주어와 be동사가 생략됨
- as: '…때문에'라는 의미의 접속사

14행   … when I heard that one narrow tunnel **leads** to another underground city ….
- leads: 들은 내용이 전달하는 시점에도 여전히 사실인 경우로, 시제 일치 법칙에 따르지 않고 현재 시제가 사용됨

15행   Despite **the many oil lamps** *burning*, I could breathe **so** comfortably **that** I almost forgot ….
- the many oil lamps: 동명사의 의미상 주어
- burning: 전치사 Despite의 목적어 역할을 하는 동명사
- so … that ~: 너무 …해서 ~하다

STRATEGIC SUMMARY   religious, maze, accommodate, connected, enormous

EXPANDING KNOWLEDGE

1 b **2** d

세계에서 가장 외딴곳에 있는 수도원 중 하나는 그리스에 있는 Meteora이다. 여러 봉우리 꼭대기에 지어진 이곳은 1988년부터 유네스코 세계 문화유산이었다.
　　Meteora는 그리스어로 '하늘 한가운데' 또는 '공중에 매달린'을 의미한다. 그런데 왜 그리고 누가 이러한 건축물을 높은 절벽 위에 자리 잡게 했을까? 11세기에 수도자들은 그 지역 동굴에 살았다. 하지만 터키가 그리스를 침략한 후, 동굴은 안전하지 않게 되었고, 수도자들은 바위 위의 더욱더 높은 곳으로 이동했다. 결국, 그들은 예배를 드리기 위한 영구적인 건물을 지을 봉우리로 이동했다. 그 당시, 수도자들은 물자와 사람을 봉우리 꼭대기로 옮기기 위해 사다리와 바구니를 이용했다. 19세기와 20세기가 되어서야 꼭대기로 가는 길이 만들어졌다.

어휘 remote[rimóut] 혱 외진, 외딴   worship[wɔ́:rʃip] 몡 예배, 숭배   peak[piːk] 몡 (산의) 봉우리
suspend[səspénd] 통 매달다   perch[pəːrtʃ] 통 (높은 곳에) 두다[앉히다]   cliff[klif] 몡 절벽

monk[mʌŋk] 몡 수도자   invade[invéid] 통 침입하다   construct[kənstrʌ́kt] 통 건설하다
permanent[pə́ːrmənənt] 톙 영구적인   conduct[kəndʌ́kt] 통 (특정한 활동을) 하다   prayer[prɛər]
몡 (*pl.*) 예배   ladder[lǽdər] 몡 사다리

구문   2행   (Having been) **Built** on the tops of several peaks, it *has been* a UNESCO World
Heritage Site since 1988.
- Built: 주절의 시제보다 앞선 때를 나타내는 완료형 분사구문으로, 앞에 Having been이 생략됨
- has been: '…해 왔다'의 의미로, 계속을 나타내는 현재완료

12행   **It was not until** the 19th and 20th centuries **that** roads [*leading* to the top]
were built.
- It is not until ... that ~: …해서야 비로소 ~하다
- leading 이하는 roads를 수식하는 현재분사구

VOCABULARY REVIEW

A   **1** conviction   **2** restrict   **3** empire   **4** heritage
B   **1** impressive   **2** permanent   **3** defend   **4** oppression   **5** endless   **6** remote
C   **1** b   **2** a

unit
20 ENVIRONMENT   pp. 84-87

★*Biodiversity*

1 b   **2** a   **3** Because a wide variety of life forms are used to produce medicine.   **4** b   **5** d
6 *1)* F   *2)* T

점점 더 많은 식물과 동물이 멸종됨에 따라, 생물 다양성, 즉 지구 상의 다양한 생물 형태가 줄어든다. 우리가 식물과 동물의 자연 서식지를 보호하기 위해 더 많은 것을 하지 않는다면, 2050년쯤에는 전체 자연 생물의 약 30퍼센트가 멸종할 것이다. 이것은 어떤 영향을 미칠까?

생물 다양성의 손실은 자연과 인간 모두에 위험한 영향을 끼칠 것이다. 지구는 하나의 거대한 기계와 같고, 이곳의 모든 생물은 서로 연관되어 있어 그 기계를 작동시키는 데 중요한 역할을 한다. 예를 들어, 토양에서 사는 벌레와 박테리아는 질소를 생산하는데, 이것은 농작물을 튼튼하게 해준다. 이 작은 생명체들이 멸종된다면, 우리는 더 이상 농작물을 제대로 재배할 수 없을 것이다. 이와 유사하게, 플랑크톤과 같은 아주 작은 바다 식물은 공기로부터 이산화탄소를 흡수한다. 만약 이러한 식물들이 멸종된다면, 호흡할 깨끗한 공기가 충분하지 않게 될 것이다.

생물 다양성은 또한 인간의 건강을 유지하는 데 중요한 역할을 한다. 매우 다양한 종류의 생물이 의약품을 생산하는 데 사용된다. 항생제를 포함해서 우리가 현재 사용하는 의약품의 4분의 1가량이 자연 유기체를 함유한다. 또한, 진통제와 페니실린 같은 많은 다른 의약품들이 자연 유기체의 분석을 통해 만들어졌다. 따라서 지구 상에 유기체가 더 적을수록, 미래에 새로운 의약품을 개발하기가 더 어려워질 것이다.

요약하면, 생물 다양성이 소실된다면 세계는 아주 다른 곳이 될 것이다. 토양에 쓰일 질소나 환자를 위한 약과 같은 것들은 공급이 고갈됨에 따라 매우 비싸질 것이며, 국가들은 그것들을 입수하기 위해 서로 경쟁해야만 할 것이다. 이것은 여러 문제들, 심지어 전쟁으로도 이어질 수 있다. 그러므로 우리가 지구의 생물 다양성을 지키기 위해 뭔가 하지 않으면 삶은 더욱 나빠질 것이다.

어휘   extinct[ikstíŋkt] 톙 멸종된   biodiversity[bàioudivə́ːrsəti] 몡 생물 다양성   decline[dikláin]
통 줄어들다, 감소하다   habitat[hǽbitæt] 몡 서식지   nitrogen[náitrədʒən] 몡 질소
strengthen[stréŋkθən] 통 강화하다, 더 튼튼하게 하다   crop[krap] 몡 (농)작물   properly[prάpərli]

🕒 제대로   absorb[æbsɔ́ːrb] 🕒 흡수하다   carbon dioxide 이산화탄소   vital[váitl] 🕒 필수적인
quarter[kwɔ́ːrtər] 🕒 4분의 1   antibiotic[æntibaiátik] 🕒 항생제   organism[ɔ́ːrgənìzm]
🕒 유기체 (microorganism 🕒 미생물)   penicillin[pènisílin] 🕒 페니실린   extremely[ikstríːmli]
🕒 매우, 극도로   supply[səplái] 🕒 공급   run low 고갈되다, 모자라게 되다   compete[kəmpíːt]
🕒 경쟁하다   access[ǽkses] 🕒 접근; *입수   [문제] conserve[kənsɔ́ːrv] 🕒 보호하다
overpopulation[òuvərpɑpjuléiʃən] 🕒 인구[개체 수] 과잉

구문　3행　**Unless** we do more to protect the natural habitats of plants and animals, ….
　　　　　• unless: …하지 않는 한(= if … not)

　　　9행　…, the worms and bacteria [**that** live in soil] produce nitrogen, *which*
strengthens crops.
　　　　　• that 이하는 the worms and bacteria를 수식하는 주격 관계대명사절
　　　　　• which: nitrogen을 보충 설명하는 계속적 용법의 주격 관계대명사(= and it)

　　　15행　Around **a quarter of the medicines** [*that* we currently use], including
antibiotics, **contain** natural organisms.
　　　　　• 부분 표현(some, most, the rest, half, 분수, 퍼센트 등) + of + 명사: 명사에 동사의 수를
일치시킴
　　　　　• that 이하는 the medicines를 수식하는 목적격 관계대명사절

　　　18행　…, **the fewer** organisms we have on Earth, **the more difficult** it will be to
develop new medicines in the future.
　　　　　• the + 비교급 …, the + 비교급 ~: …하면 할수록 더 ~하다

　　　21행　…, **if** biodiversity **were** lost, the world **would be** a very different place.
　　　　　• if + 주어 + 동사의 과거형[were], 주어 + 조동사의 과거형 + 동사원형: 가정법 과거

STRATEGIC SUMMARY　nature, extinct, analysis, lack, compete

EXPANDING KNOWLEDGE

1 c　**2** *1)* T　*2)* T

우리는 북극과 남극이 북극곰과 펭귄만이 살아남을 수 있는, 텅 비고 생명체가 살지 않는 곳이라고 생각하지만,
현재 200종이 넘는 다양한 생물 종이 그곳에 살고 있다. 사실, 남극의 생물 다양성 수준은 갈라파고스 제도보다
높은데, 갈라파고스 제도는 그곳에 서식하는 다양한 생물 종으로 유명하다. 북극과 남극에서 과학자들은 고래와 새,
벌레, 그리고 다른 여러 동물들을 발견했다. 그들은 지구 온난화로 인해 동물들이 더 시원한 서식지를 찾기 때문에
이 지역으로 이동하고 있다고 생각한다. 게다가, 빙하가 녹으면서 일부 바다는 현재 십만 년 만에 처음으로 햇빛에
노출되어 있다. 전 세계에서 온 과학자들은 바다 생물을 연구하고 해양에 대해 더 많은 것을 알기 위해 첨단 기술을
사용하고 있다. 극지방의 생물에 대해서는 알아야 할 정보가 무궁무진하다.

어휘　Arctic[áːrktik] 🕒 북극   Antarctic[æntáːrktik] 🕒 남극   lifeless[láiflis] 🕒 생명체가 살지 않는
polar bear 북극곰   range[reindʒ] 🕒 범위   be exposed to …에 노출되다   melt[melt] 🕒 녹다
high-tech[háiték] 🕒 첨단의   pole[poul] 🕒 (지구의) 극

구문　1행　Although we **think of** the Arctic and Antarctic **as** empty, lifeless places [*where*
only polar bears and penguins can survive], ….
　　　　　• think of A as B: A를 B라고 여기다
　　　　　• where 이하는 empty, lifeless places를 수식하는 관계부사절

VOCABULARY REVIEW

A　**1** breathe　**2** habitat　**3** antibiotic　**4** analysis
B　**1** range　**2** lifeless　**3** extinct　**4** compete　**5** species　**6** absorb
C　**1** a　**2** c

MEMO

MEMO

MEMO

MEMO